What Life Was Like®

IN EUROPE'S GOLDEN AGE

Northern Europe
AD 1500 ~ 1675

What Life Was Like

IN EUROPE'S GOLDEN AGE

Northern Europe
AD 1500 ~ 1675

BY THE EDITORS OF TIME-LIFE BOOKS, ALEXANDRIA, VIRGINIA

CONTENTS

Reform, Revolt, and Riches:
Overview and Timeline   8

1

Birth of the Reformation   14

2

Peasants and Princes Battle for Freedom   62

3

Amsterdam, the "Golden Swamp"   108

ESSAYS

Dürer's Door   52

The World's Marketplace   98

Much Loved Dutch Children   150

GLOSSARY   158
PRONUNCIATION GUIDE   160
ACKNOWLEDGMENTS   161
PICTURE CREDITS   161
BIBLIOGRAPHY   162
INDEX   164

In Europe's Golden Age

Reform, Revolt, and Riches

In 1517 an obscure German monk named Martin Luther sought a scholarly debate on certain practices of the Roman Catholic Church. The church, which had long been the most influential institution in Europe, suffered from corruption at the hands of members of its hierarchy and, over the years, reformers frequently called for change. But to Luther's great surprise, his action ignited a firestorm of religious, political, and social rebellion that burned through Germany, into the Netherlands, and eventually throughout Europe. In 1518 the Catholic Church moved to silence Luther's criticisms, but its opposition only fanned the flames. From the resulting conflagration would be born not only a new religious pluralism—new sects such as the Anabaptists, Mennonites, Calvinists, Huguenots, and others lumped under the heading of Protestantism would sprout and flourish—but also a golden age of commerce and culture.

The bold ideas and ideals of the Italian Renaissance had been moving northward for some time, and Germany and the Netherlands, or Low Countries, were ripe for such a revolution. On the religious front, the two lands had already embraced Christian humanism, whose proponents, such as Erasmus, emphasized individual spirituality. Politically, German and Netherlands leaders were accustomed to a large measure of autonomy. Though under the rule of the same sovereign, both countries comprised many politically independent territories and cities. Their leaders, strong-minded German and Netherlands princes and electors, chafed under the yoke of rule from afar.

1505
Martin Luther joins the Augustinian order

1516
Erasmus publishes first edition of the New Testament in Greek

1517
Luther issues his Ninety-five Theses against indulgences in Wittenberg, Saxony

1518
Luther is interrogated by the papal legate Dominican cardinal Cajetan, in Augsburg, Bavaria

1519
Luther rejects primacy of pope; the Holy Roman Emperor Maximilian I dies and his grandson Charles V is named emperor

1521
Luther is excommunicated by Pope Leo X; Charles V issues Edict of Worms, declaring Luther an outlaw

1524-1526
Landgrave Philip of Hesse converts to Lutheranism; the German Peasants' War occurs

1529
The Diet of Speyer reaffirms the Edict of Worms; Lutheran princes and cities protest enforcement of it, giving rise to the term Protestant

1530
Lutheran leaders present statement of their religious beliefs, the Augsburg Confession, to Charles V; the Diet of Augsburg proscribes all heresy and reaffirms the Edict of Worms

The focus of their discontent was Charles V, who as Holy Roman emperor and king of Spain was overlord of Germany and sovereign of the 17 Netherlands provinces. When he ascended the imperial throne in 1519, Charles considered himself not only ruler of the farthest-flung empire the world had ever known—consisting of much of Europe as well as territories in Asia, Africa, and the Americas—but also "God's standard-bearer," defender of the Roman Catholic faith. Eager for complete autonomy, ambitious territorial rulers and city officials used the growing religious conflicts to distance themselves from Charles; they converted to Lutheranism and began to oppose both the emperor's and the pope's policies.

During the 1530s, Germany's Protestant leaders formed the Schmalkaldic League, an alliance dedicated to defending its members from the emperor. Determined to quash insurgency, Charles defeated the league in 1547. And in the Netherlands, his Spanish inquisitors vigorously hunted down heretics. But the tide turned against him when one of his key German supporters defected and led a successful revolt against him. Under the resulting peace agreement, the German princes were granted the right to decide the religious preference, Lutheranism or Catholicism, of their lands.

That same year, Charles V abdicated his rule over the Low Countries in favor of his son, Philip. But Philip, too, used a heavy-handed approach to suppress heresy and centralize government in the Netherlands. His political policies antagonized the nobles, cities, and provin-

1531

Protestant German princes and cities form defensive military alliance, the Schmalkaldic League

1534

First complete edition of Luther's translation of the Bible

1536

John Calvin publishes the first edition of the *Institutes of the Christian Religion* and subsequently assumes leadership of the Genevan Reformation

1540

Society of Jesus approved by the pope, part of Rome's effort at Counter Reformation

1546

Death of Martin Luther

1547

Battle of Mühlberg; Charles V smashes the Schmalkaldic League

1552

Lutheran princes revolt against Charles V

1555

The Peace of Augsburg provides for Germany's rulers to decide the religion of their subjects; Philip of Spain becomes Netherlands ruler

1556

Charles V turns over the Spanish throne to Philip and abdicates the crown of Holy Roman emperor in favor of his brother, Ferdinand

cial estates, or governing bodies, while at the same time he angered a strong new sect of Protestant opponents, the Calvinists.

In 1566, pushed to the breaking point, Calvinists across the Netherlands rioted, smashing images in the Catholic churches. An infuriated Philip sent the duke of Alva to quell this new revolt. Galvanized by the show of force, the Dutch fought back under the leadership of William, prince of Orange, who had served as Philip's stadholder, or governor, for the provinces of Holland, Zeeland, and Utrecht. William's goal was to liberate both the predominantly Catholic southern provinces and the more Protestant northern provinces. In 1576 the States-General of the Netherlands assumed control of the government, and all 17 provinces agreed to unite against the Spanish. But this unity would not last, in part because of the Calvinists' unyielding demand for the total abolition of Catholicism. By 1579 most of the southern Netherlands had been recovered for Spain.

Both Philip and William engaged in political maneuverings to win the war, which continued unabated. In 1580 the Spanish king declared William of Orange an outlaw and encouraged would-be assassins to destroy the rebellion by killing the prince. Philip's ploy succeeded—but only in part. In 1584 William fell to an assassin's bullet, but the war raged on. Under the leadership of William's son Maurice, the Dutch Republic, assisted intermittently by England and France, fought Spain to a standoff; a 12-year truce was negotiated in 1609.

This temporary peace allowed the United Provinces to thrive. The

1564
Death of John Calvin

1566
A coalition of Netherlands nobles protests Spanish heresy laws; Calvinists hold open-air preachings and destroy images in Catholic churches

1567
The Spanish duke of Alva arrives in the Netherlands to put down the rebellion and establishes the Council of Troubles

1568
Eighty years of warring between the Netherlands and Spain begins; William of Orange leads an unsuccessful rebellion

1580
Philip II proclaims William of Orange an outlaw and offers a reward to his captor or assassin

1581
The States-General of the Netherlands renounces the authority of Philip II

1584
William of Orange is assassinated at Delft; subsequently, his son Maurice becomes stadholder of Holland and Zeeland

1602
The Dutch East India Company is founded

1606
Rembrandt van Rijn is born in Leiden

17th century became a golden age for the Netherlands—politically, socially, and financially. The republic's streets teemed with traders from exotic ports, prosperous merchants, and adventurers bound for Dutch colonies in the East and West Indies. The arts and sciences flourished, particularly in the great city of Amsterdam, home to some of the world's most renowned artists, such as Rembrandt van Rijn.

While other European governments were becoming absolutist and were dominated by their aristocracies, the Dutch lived in a republic with no single seat of power. Each province was self-governing, sending delegates to a central States-General to settle the republic's collective interests. In 1650 the stadholdership traditionally held by the princes of Orange was abandoned by the five leading provinces following an attempted coup by stadholder William II. Thereafter, leadership of the country fell to Holland and the city of Amsterdam.

Over the next 20 years, the republic battled England and France over trade, colonial possessions, and territory. In 1672 the country faced its greatest crisis as England battered the United Provinces on the sea and the French seized control of three provinces. In desperation, the Dutch turned to then prince of Orange William III, naming him stadholder of Holland and Zeeland and prince-captain of the republic. He quickly helped evict the invaders. But the fighting had taken its toll. The economy was crippled, and the Dutch lost their prominence on the world stage. Yet theirs had been a glorious reign, a golden age made possible by the chain of events set in motion by an unknown monk.

1609
A 12-year truce between Spain and the Dutch Republic begins

1621
The Dutch West India Company is chartered; war with Spain resumes

1648
Spain recognizes Dutch independence in the Treaty of Münster, ending eight decades of intermittent warfare

1650
William II lays siege to Amsterdam but dies soon after, ushering in a period of republican government for five Dutch provinces

1652-1654
The first Anglo-Dutch war occurs, growing out of the commercial rivalry between the two countries

1665-1667
The second Anglo-Dutch war is fought in the North Sea, off Africa, and in North America and the West Indies

1667-1668
French king Louis XIV invades the Spanish Netherlands

1672
The third Anglo-Dutch war breaks out; Louis XIV's army invades the Dutch Republic; the Amsterdam stock exchange crashes. William III becomes stadholder, ending the period of republican rule

1689
William III and Mary Stuart become king and queen of England

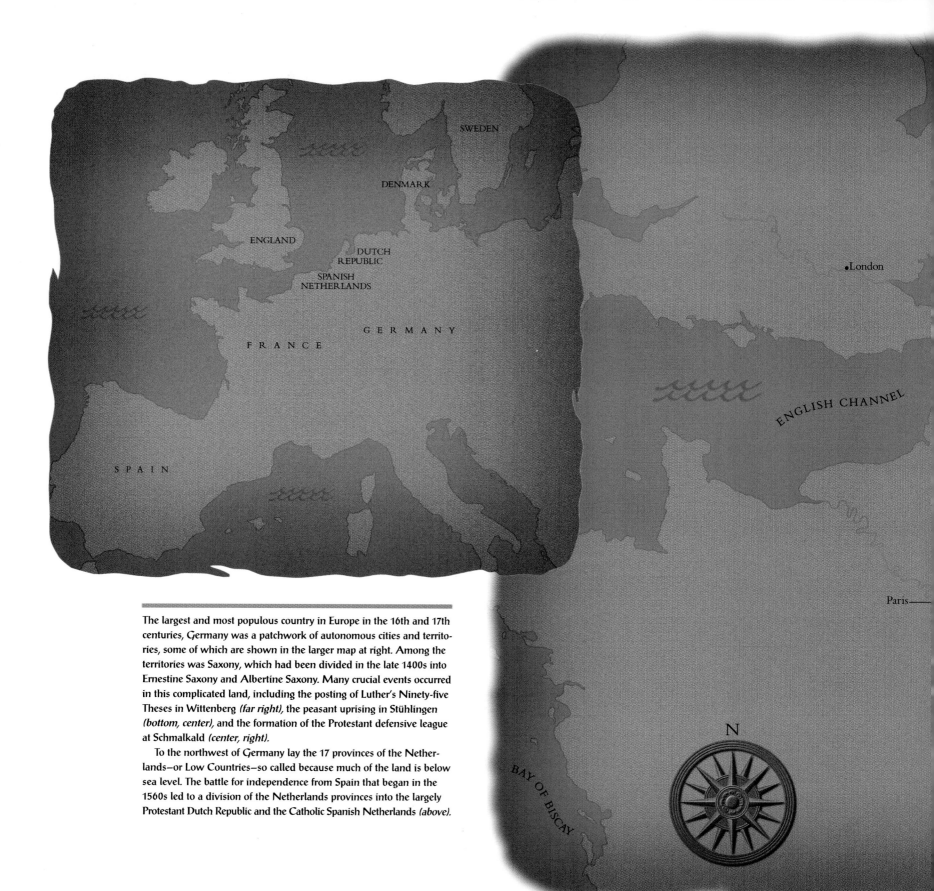

SWEDEN

DENMARK

ENGLAND

DUTCH
REPUBLIC

SPANISH
NETHERLANDS

GERMANY

FRANCE

SPAIN

•London

ENGLISH CHANNEL

Paris

The largest and most populous country in Europe in the 16th and 17th centuries, Germany was a patchwork of autonomous cities and territories, some of which are shown in the larger map at right. Among the territories was Saxony, which had been divided in the late 1400s into Ernestine Saxony and Albertine Saxony. Many crucial events occurred in this complicated land, including the posting of Luther's Ninety-five Theses in Wittenberg *(far right)*, the peasant uprising in Stühlingen *(bottom, center)*, and the formation of the Protestant defensive league at Schmalkald *(center, right)*.

To the northwest of Germany lay the 17 provinces of the Netherlands—or Low Countries—so called because much of the land is below sea level. The battle for independence from Spain that began in the 1560s led to a division of the Netherlands provinces into the largely Protestant Dutch Republic and the Catholic Spanish Netherlands *(above)*.

N

BAY OF BISCAY

NORTH SEA

BALTIC SEA

Stralsund

GRONINGEN

Hamburg

FRIESLAND

BRANDENBURG

HOLLAND

ZUIDER ZEE

Elbe River

Haarlem

Amsterdam

Leiden

The Hague

UTRECHT

GELDERLAND

The Brill

Gouda

Rotterdam

ZEELAND

Vlissingen

Rhine River

Münster

Wittenberg

Antwerp

Torgau

FLANDERS

Ghent

BRABANT

Meuse River

SAXONY

Scheldt River

Brussels

Tournai

Cologne

HESSE

Mühlhausen

Leipzig

Mühlberg

Eisenach

Erfurt

Marburg

NASSAU

Schmalkald

LUXEMBOURG

Frankfurt

Trier

Mainz

Worms

PALATINATE

Heidelberg

Speyer

Nürnberg

Strasbourg

WÜRTTEMBERG

BAVARIA

Augsburg

Munich

Memmingen

Lech River

Basel

Stühlingen

Konstanz

Lake Constance

Zürich

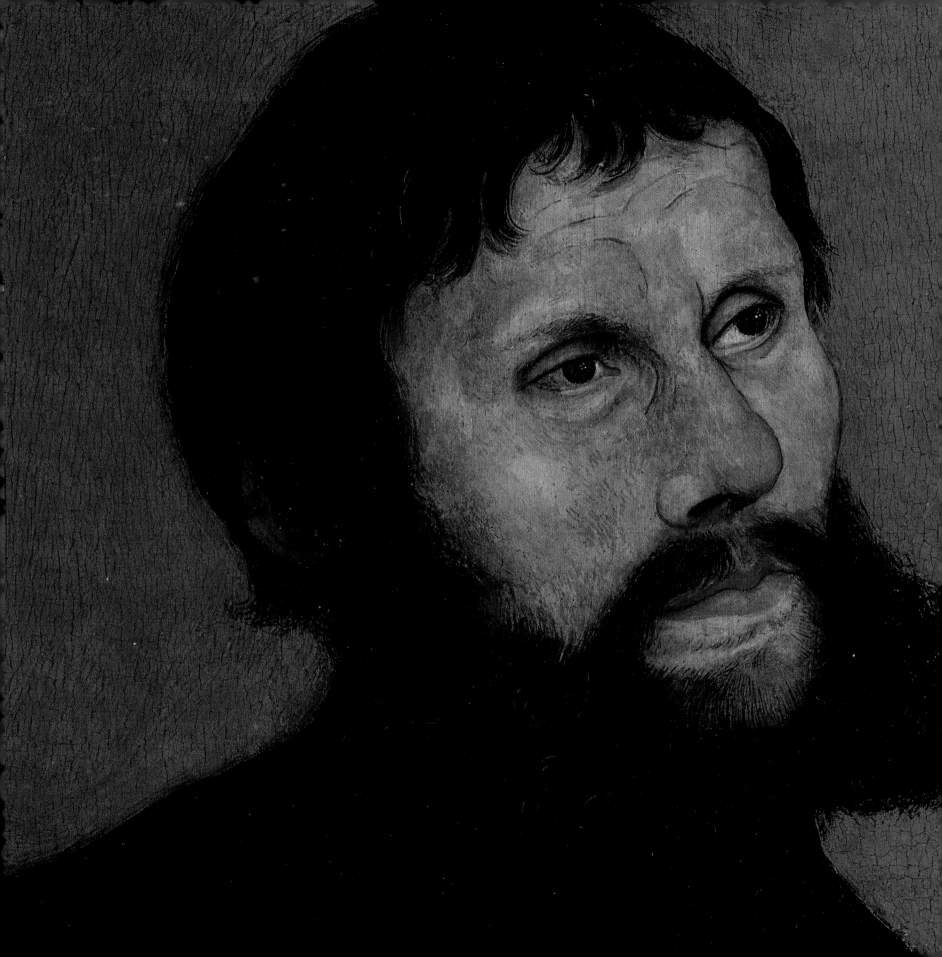

CHAPTER ONE

Birth of the Reformation

Condemned as a heretic by the pope and branded an outlaw by the Holy Roman emperor in 1521, monk and Reformer Martin Luther grew his hair and beard long to disguise himself as an imperial knight *(left)*. Luther's beliefs and actions would inspire the Reformation and splinter the Western Church.

xhausted, sick, and fearful, on October 7, 1518, Martin Luther entered the Bavarian city of Augsburg, where he had been summoned by the Catholic Church to answer accusations of heresy—a crime punishable by death. Traveling most of the way from his home in Wittenberg, Saxony, by foot, the Augustinian monk had covered some 325 miles in just 12 days.

It had been a harrowing journey. Not only had Luther been striving to reach Augsburg in the time allotted by the church, but whenever he had stopped to rest at one of the small hamlets that dotted the German countryside, anxious supporters had expressed concern for his safety. Foremost in the minds of some was the fate of Jan Hus, a Czech religious leader who, like Luther, had challenged church practices. In 1414 Hus had been invited to attend the church's Council of Konstanz, where, despite a safe-conduct pass, he was seized, tried for heresy, and burned at the stake. "They will burn you," Luther's fellow monks warned as he drew ever closer to Augsburg. "Turn back."

Luther could not retreat from the path ahead. In the preceding years he had become more and more troubled about certain issues; this was his opportunity to discuss them. He knew the situation was dangerous. The Catholic Church had great influence in the Holy Roman Empire, which included, among many others, the German states of Bavaria and Saxony. But Luther bolstered his courage with the knowledge that he had the powerful support of Frederick the Wise, elector of Saxony. It was the elector who had persuaded the church to hold Luther's hearing on German soil, rather than in Rome, where, like Hus, Luther would almost certainly have been imprisoned, tried, and executed without delay. Here Luther had friends, and he might yet be saved from the church's wrath.

The controversy surrounding Luther stemmed from the church's practice of selling letters of indulgence. Indulgences remitted penalties for sins that were unrepented (unconfessed) or unsatisfied (penance such as fasting or pilgrimages had not been performed), so that when a Christian died he or she would not have to suffer in purgatory in order to be purified of these sins. In the 11th century, indulgences had been granted freely during the First Crusade to crusaders, so that they would not die with such sins still on their souls while fighting for Christ in a distant land. Only later were letters of indulgence sold to allay anxiety about purgatorial punishment for failure to perform penance.

As the centuries passed, the church sold ever more indulgences to meet its rising need for money to erect churches and to fund its own internal expansionary wars ("holy crusades" against dissenting groups and hostile rulers such as the king of Naples). By Luther's time, concerned relatives could even buy a reduction of the time spent in purgatory by a deceased loved one. Jan Hus had protested such practices. Others deplored them as well, and by the 16th century, the selling of indulgences for such purposes had become the subject of biting satire.

According to legend, Frederick *(inset)* dreamed of Luther's October 31, 1517, posting of the Ninety-five Theses the night before. In the dream *(above)*, Luther inscribes his theses on the church door with a pen that stretches from Wittenberg to Rome, where it impales a lion and strikes the crown from the head of a man, figures that represent Pope Leo X. Also portrayed are the burning of 15th-century religious protester Jan Hus *(top left)* and a white swan, signifying Luther's purity and sacrifice.

Luther's objections, spelled out in his Ninety-five Theses, were threefold. First, the most recent and blatant abuses arose from the massive sale of indulgences for the rebuilding of St. Peter's basilica in Rome. "The revenues of all Christendom are being sucked into this insatiable basilica," Luther charged. Second, he objected to the notion that the pope had power over purgatory, which Luther believed only God possessed. "If the pope does have the power to release anyone from purgatory," Luther demanded, "why in the name of love does he not abolish purgatory by letting everyone out?" Finally, as a pastor charged with the spiritual well-being of his flock, Luther believed indulgences to be "positively harmful" to the naive recipient. "Those persons are damned," Luther declared, "who think that letters of indulgence make them certain of salvation." Rather—according to Luther's reading of a crucial passage in the Bible—salvation is God's gift freely bestowed on those who have faith, a state of grace that cannot be bought and sold for money or even for good deeds.

As tradition has it, Luther nailed a copy of the Theses to the door of the castle church, also known as the Church of All Saints, in Wittenberg on October 31, 1517. Such an action would not have been unusual, since announcements for public events were frequently nailed to the church's door, and Luther was only seeking open scholarly debate on the issue. He claimed—in those days—to have no thought of undermining church or papal authority. But without Luther's knowledge, the Theses were translated into German from their original Latin by humanists critical of church doctrine, and they were widely published by the many printing presses that had sprung up in recent decades. Within just a few months, Martin Luther's work had been distributed all over the Continent, cap-

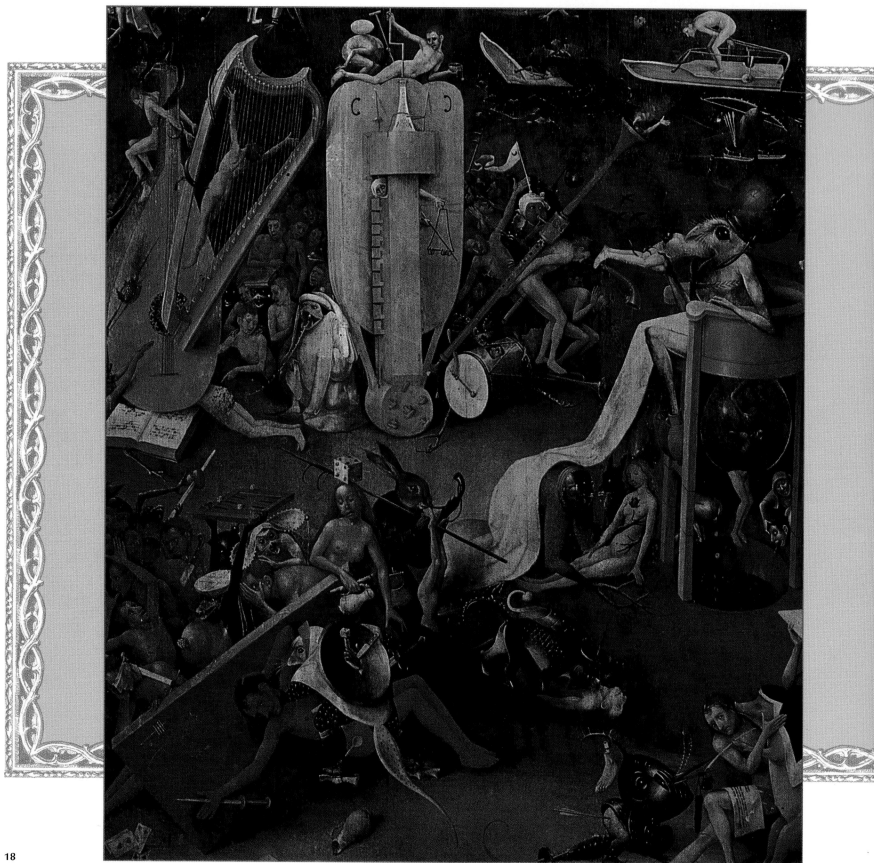

The dead are tormented for their sins in this vision of hell *(left)* by Dutch painter Hieronymus Bosch. Monsters bearing dice and cards attack gamblers, while musical instruments torture those who have lived frivolous lives. Gluttonous souls are eaten, then excreted.

Two clergymen sell indulgences while the pope, on horseback, watches the transactions near a cross from which more indulgences hang, signifying the Roman church's approval of the practice.

Indulgences for Sale

God's wrath and eternal damnation were concepts both real and terrifying to Luther's contemporaries. The prospect of hell, where those with unrepented and unforgiven mortal sins suffered endlessly, or purgatory, where the guilty-but-saved paid painful but temporary penalties for lesser sins, was horrific. The church counted on the fear of hell to instill discipline and obedience among the faithful. But once sins were committed, the faithful could resort to the sacrament of penance, where the priest transformed eternal penalties into good works, such as prayers, pilgrimages, and fasting, that could be done in the here and now to absolve the transgression.

To be on the safe side, Christians afraid of dying with sins not satisfied by penance could purchase a letter of indulgence to keep themselves out of purgatory or to free departed relatives already suffering there. As a bonus, people were treated to a traveling sideshow by the indulgence sellers. Dominican preacher Johann Tetzel, for example, hawked his papal wares in small towns and villages in Brandenburg and ducal Saxony, spicing his appearances with grand processions and rousing sermons. On one occasion, he cried from the pulpit, "Don't you hear the voices of your wailing dead parents and others who say, 'Have mercy upon me, have mercy upon me, because we are in severe punishment and pain. From this you could redeem us with a small alms.'" A catchier line attributed to Tetzel went: "As soon as the coin in the coffer rings, the soul from Purgatory springs."

Tetzel sold indulgences on the borders of electoral Saxony, where Luther lived, in April 1517. Hearing of the preacher's antics helped inspire Luther to pen his Ninety-five Theses condemning the practice. Of Tetzel himself, Luther later wrote, "With might and main he sold grace for money as dearly or as cheaply as he could."

turing the attention of princes and peasants, artists and clergy. The Wittenberg professor had ignited a firestorm.

The church, at first dismissive of the lowly monk, grew alarmed. Luther's persistence in his criticism of church practices—and with it papal authority—represented an intolerable threat. Even the Holy Roman emperor, Maximilian I, regarded Luther's teachings as subversive. And so Luther was summoned first to Rome and then, with Frederick's intervention, to Augsburg instead.

There being no Augustinian monastery in Augsburg, Frederick had arranged for Luther to be housed at the Carmelite cloister. Despite a severe stomach ailment, Luther quickly sent word of his arrival to the Dominican cardinal Cajetan of Thiene, before whom he was scheduled to appear. But Luther's various advisers in Augsburg, whose support had been arranged by Frederick's secretary and chaplain, Georg Spalatin, were appalled to learn that Luther had entered the lion's den without obtaining an imperial safe-conduct. Without such a document, they argued, there was nothing to stop Cajetan from seizing Luther immediately and transporting him to Rome. (Unbeknown to Luther or his advisers, Frederick had already extracted a promise from Cajetan that the monk would not be taken.) The imperial counselors eventually supplied the guarantee, and on October 12 Luther left the relative safety of the Carmelite cloister to face his papal judge.

The meeting took place at the palace of the powerful Fugger banking family, a sumptuous residence that outshone anything owned by the Holy Roman emperor. Luther had been instructed on how to behave at this first encounter with the pope's emissary. Upon entering the room, he fell prostrate on the floor at the cardinal's feet. There he waited until Cajetan had bidden him three times to rise.

Studying the man before him, Cajetan saw a heavy-boned yet emaciated figure whose face was dominated by a set of dark, fiery eyes. He was dressed simply, in the black cowl of his order. Attired in the magnificent red robes and red hat of a

In October 1518 Cardinal Cajetan *(right)* interrogates Luther about suspected heresies. Afterward, Cajetan urged Frederick the Wise, elector of Saxony, either to "have the monk Martin sent to Rome or to chase him from Your lands. Your Highness should not let one little friar bring such ignominy over You and Your house."

Catholic cardinal, the small and delicate Cajetan presented a sharp contrast to Luther. Cardinal Cajetan reveled in the trappings of his office and the pomp and circumstance that accompanied his comings and goings; he was attended at the hearing by a group of Italian courtiers.

Encouraged by Luther's humble manner, the cardinal hoped for a quick recantation. Addressing the monk as "dear son," Caj-

etan told him that the pope demanded three things: Luther must retract his errors, promise to abstain from such statements in the future, and never again disturb the church.

Luther was stunned. "I could just as well have done these things at Wittenberg without exposing myself to danger," he would later write. He had expected an opportunity to discuss the issues that troubled him. He would recant nothing without first being shown where he had erred, Luther insisted to the cardinal, and the refutation must come not from papal authority but from the Scriptures.

Cajetan faced a dilemma. He had been specifically forbidden by the pope to enter into any sort of disputation with Luther. But the cardinal was one of the most learned theologians in all of Christendom and was certain he could show this misguided monk his errors in thinking and interpretation. So against his orders, Cajetan engaged Luther in debate.

For three days the Dominican cardinal and the Augustinian monk argued and defended their positions. Luther's scholarship was impeccable and his knowledge of the Bible thorough, and he knew enough Greek and Hebrew to judge any interpretations. Cajetan was equally intelligent and learned. But each man's arguments turned on at least one essential question on whose answer they disagreed: Which took precedence, papal law or Scripture?

Luther essentially dismissed papal bulls—decrees issued by the pope, in this case ones supporting the issue of indulgences—as so much evidence of papal fallibility, in contrast to the certain authority of Scripture. He declared that salvation came to individuals through God's grace only, independent of the pope, which was why indulgences were nothing more than a vile money-making scheme. For Luther to recant would thus be going against his conscience, since he was utterly convinced that his interpretation of the Scriptures was divine truth.

Cajetan reminded Luther that the church was a powerful

enemy. "Do you think the pope cares about Germany? Do you imagine the princes will defend you with arms?"

"No," the monk said.

If the church excommunicated Luther, Cajetan warned, no one would shelter him. "Where will you stay?"

Luther replied simply, "Under the sky."

The proceedings were at an insurmountable impasse. Cajetan dismissed the monk. "Begone," he said. "Either revoke or come not again into my presence." He would have nothing further to do with Luther, calling him "the beast with deep-seated eyes" who had "strange ideas flitting through his head."

Luther, for his part, held the cardinal in equal contempt, regarding Cajetan's statements as heretical and writing later that his theological skill was on a par with that of an ass playing the lute. As he told Andreas Karlstadt, a fellow Wittenberg professor and theologian: "He

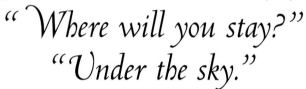

"*Where will you stay?*"
"*Under the sky.*"

will hear nothing from me except 'I recant, I revoke, I confess that I erred,' which I would not say."

For three days Luther waited to be summoned again. From the cardinal there was only silence. Rumors reached Luther that he would be arrested. On the advice of one of his counselors, the Augustinian monk wrote to Cajetan on October 17 to apologize for not having been properly deferential. He wrote again the next day to tell the cardinal he was leaving Augsburg—and then waited, with growing anxiety, for a response.

As the silence grew increasingly ominous, Luther's friends took matters into their own hands. On the night of October 20, they plucked Luther from his room at the cloister and spirited him out of the city. So abruptly was he taken that he found him-

self astride a horse, riding all night in only his knee breeches and stockings. Eleven days later, on October 31, Martin Luther arrived back at the Augustinian monastery in Wittenberg. It was the first anniversary of the Ninety-five Theses.

The man who would prove instrumental in shattering the structure of the medieval Catholic Church lived and worked at a time when reform was on the lips of many, in both the religious and the secular spheres. In 1453 Constantinople had fallen to the Turks, and a number of scholarly Greeks sought refuge in southern Europe, bringing with them the heritage of classical antiquity. As European scholars turned a fresh eye to the New Testament, they found discrepancies between the earlier versions, written in Greek, and the Latin Bible that had been accepted by the church since the sixth century. By 1500 theologians in northern Europe were experimenting with new practices and ideas that they believed agreed more faithfully with the old truths—thereby undermining or discrediting much of traditional church authority.

Meanwhile, there were growing political problems in the religious-political entity known as the Holy Roman Empire, which had been established in the 10th century in an effort to bring Christian unity to Europe. By the 16th century, the empire had grown largely German in both language and location and was controlled in large part by powerful German princes. They exercised considerable authority over the emperor, who was elected not by the pope but by the seven electoral states. Four of these states were secular and were recognized as autonomous political dynasties—Bohemia, Brandenburg, Palatinate, and Saxony.

Erasmus, Christian Humanist

The most influential of the northern Renaissance humanists—scholars who studied the classical Greek and Latin texts—was Dutchman Desiderius Erasmus. Erasmus produced a large body of work, ranging from classical scholarship to collections of proverbs, but his satires proved to be his most popular pieces. These works attacked abuses in the state and the church and mocked scholars and theologians, a "touchy lot." His brilliant *The Praise of Folly*, a look at the absurdity of human behavior, went through 42 editions in Latin between 1509 and 1536. His writings incensed church officials, but in the years of relative tolerance before the Reformation, the church did not move against him.

Erasmus avoided taking sides in the bitter debate between the Reformers and the Catholic Church. In March 1519 Martin Luther tried to enlist his support. Erasmus told Luther, "Old institutions cannot be uprooted in an instant. Quiet argument may do more than wholesale condemnation. Avoid all appearances of sedition. Keep cool. Do not get angry. Do not hate anybody." But Erasmus also defended Luther, warning the church against intolerance.

Erasmus's refusal to break with the church while at the same time refusing to condemn the Reformer earned him few friends. Catholics turned against him, saying he had "laid the egg which Luther hatched." And Luther later dismissed Erasmus as a dreamer who "thinks that all can be accomplished with civility and benevolence."

Erasmus sat for this 1523 portrait, by Hans Holbein the Younger, in Basel, Switzerland. For a while, he found refuge there from the political and religious turmoil of the Reformation.

(Saxony was an unusual case, having been divided in 1485 between two brothers, Ernest and Albert. Ernestine Saxony, then under Frederick the Wise, was an electoral state; Albertine Saxony, under Duke George, was not.) The remaining three electoral states were ecclesiastical—the archbishoprics of Cologne, Trier, and Mainz. In addition to the electoral states, the empire included numerous nonelectoral principalities and some 75 imperial "free cities," such as Konstanz. In short, the Holy Roman Empire was a patchwork of more than 300 sovereign principalities. Individuals considered themselves Saxons, Nürnbergers, or Bohemians, who owed allegiance first and foremost to their prince or to their city government rather than to the emperor.

By the time Luther's Ninety-five Theses was published, a number of these principalities were growing increasingly aggrieved by what they considered the pope's unwarranted intrusion into German affairs. Rome flouted German law, transferring lawsuits from German to Roman courts and forcing laypeople to stand trial in church courts under threat of excommunication. Another bitter pill was the way Rome awarded church offices and benefices, the financial "livings" of the clergy, to the highest bidder; the result was that German parishes were saddled with, as one document put it, "unqualified, unlearned, and unfit" non-Germans who failed to perform their duties and deprived the German people of proper spiritual care.

Also galling was the never-ending flow of German money into Roman coffers. Besides collecting the money paid for an office by its new occupant, the pope also collected the office's first year's income, or annate, from the Germans. He charged money to absolve certain high sins and crimes as well. Worst of all was the sale of indulgences.

German artisans stamp out silver coins, which came in a variety of currencies in the Holy Roman Empire, where every sovereign ruler was free to mint his or her own money. During the 16th century, silver replaced gold as the standard of payment, a boon for German mines, the largest producers of silver in Europe.

THE HOUSE OF FUGGER

Jacob Fugger stands before his bookkeeper Matthaus Schwartz, who painted the office scene below in 1516. On the cabinet behind the men are the names of the cities in which the Fugger family had bank branches, including Rome, Kraków, and Lisbon. Other family businesses included mines, factories, and farms.

The Fuggers monopolized the Catholic Church's financial dealings in Germany and participated in the sale of church offices and indulgences. When Albrecht of Brandenburg, archbishop and elector of Mainz, needed money to purchase a third office (which was illegal), he turned to the Fuggers. He was not the only ruler to do so. In a letter to Charles V demanding payment of a loan, Jacob Fugger reminded the emperor, "Your Majesty could not have secured the Roman Crown without me."

Thus, Luther's seeds of dissent fell on fertile ground, and from those seeds would grow the Reformation. Soon, the very tenor and texture of daily life would be transformed. In the 1520s, monks and nuns, in large numbers, would begin abandoning the cloister and marrying. A host of traditional practices of both clergy and laity would either fall by the wayside or be radically modified to fit the new biblical teaching, among them oral confession, Lenten fasting, the prohibition of foods, and the veneration of saints and images. Within a few decades, Western Christendom would show its first splinterings, followed by an official, legal separation into Catholic and Protestant camps in 1555.

The catalyst for this earth-shattering revolution was but one man. A man who, in 1517, when it all began, thought of himself as merely "a young doctor, fresh from the forge, passionately absorbed in the Holy Scriptures."

Upon returning to Wittenberg, Luther again took up his duties as professor of theology at the university. Wittenberg, in the flat northern lowlands of Saxony, was not a particularly attractive spot. One of Luther's fellow monks once characterized the town as being "on the very borderland of civilization." Travelers who followed the Elbe River on its way north would come to a sharp westward bend marked by a large hill of white sand, a stopping place that had gradually developed into a market town, appropriately named Wittenberg, or White Mountain.

Although it lay on a trade route of sorts and had a bridge across the Elbe, Wittenberg was largely surrounded by agriculture and as a trading center was significant only to the immediate region. Luther once declared from the pulpit in Wittenberg, "Our land is very sandy, in fact none other than mere stones, for it is not a fertile soil; yet God gives us daily from these stones good wine, delicious cereals; but because this miracle happens constantly, we fail to appreciate it."

From the river, which formed the town's southern bound-

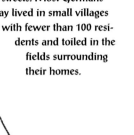

In this 16th-century German village, townspeople drink, pursue love affairs, talk with friends, and transact business. At the church, a couple publicly declares marriage vows after a procession, complete with musicians, through the streets. Most Germans of the day lived in small villages with fewer than 100 residents and toiled in the fields surrounding their homes.

ary, the outer breastworks, deep moat, strong walls, and well-fortified gates that served as watchtowers were an imposing sight. A visitor entering by the south gate would soon pass by a large house on the corner owned by the artist Lucas Cranach, who had converted the center of the house into an art studio, where at one time some 40 art students could be found. Luther spent many evenings visiting the eminent artist and perhaps sitting for portraits.

Wittenberg was a typical town for the period, even a bit larger than the average walled town of the region. With a population of no more than 2,500, the town numbered roughly 400 houses—actually, little more than squat wood cabins and mud cottages roofed with hay and straw. The town was about eight blocks long, with streets laid out at right angles to the old marketplace. Local commerce consisted of guilds of butchers, clothiers, shoemakers, and bakers, although in later years book publishing rose to some significance. There was a drugstore, owned by Cranach, which in addition to pharmaceuticals, sold spices, wax, paper, and paint. There were three public baths and also a *Frauenhaus*, or brothel, which only single persons were allowed to enter. (Luther and others succeeded in having it closed in 1521.)

Several times a week, the open marketplace was a scene of colorful activity as farmers from the countryside would bring in their wares. Twice a year the farmers' market grew into a medieval-style fair, during which some of the artisan guilds would present plays. Most of the marketplace and some of the main streets were paved and kept fairly clean and in good repair. Normally the town square was dark at night, so that citizens had to carry lanterns to avoid stepping into the streams on either side that had been diverted through the town to provide water during a siege.

As unprepossessing as Wittenberg might seem, Frederick the Wise had made it the capital of electoral Saxony and in 1490 had begun a concerted effort to beautify it. By the time Luther arrived in 1511, Frederick had completely rebuilt the castle and the castle church into a beautiful Gothic structure and assigned well-known artists, including Cranach and Albrecht Dürer, to decorate the interior. The castle church was also the home of the All Saints' Foundation, and here Frederick kept his extensive collection of saints' relics.

The relics were Frederick's passion. He had spent a lifetime collecting such items as the shred of a garment purported to have been worn by John the Baptist and a twig said to be from the burning bush of Moses. By 1518 the collection comprised some 19,000 pieces, displayed in beautiful gold, silver, and marble cases along 12 aisles. Vast throngs of the faithful would visit the gallery of the castle church (where the relics were displayed for special public viewings) to expiate their sins by praying before these shrines and purchasing indulgences associated with them. It was thus with some initial ambivalence that Frederick agreed to Luther's insistence that the sale of indulgences be stopped.

Frederick was a pious man, generally shy and cautious. As a political precaution, all of his communication with Luther was through Georg Spalatin rather than face to face. Yet the Saxon elector would prove a surprisingly tenacious ally, using as leverage the political power that belonged to him as the ruler of one of the seven electoral states. Frederick supported Luther to safeguard Saxon authority from encroachment by Rome and to maintain the reputation of the University of Wittenberg. Wisely, he also recognized that Luther's popular support was such as to threaten an outbreak of public protests should any harm befall the monk.

That Luther held a respected position as a university professor and that he was causing such controversy in the wider world was a source of wonder to one who often referred to himself as the son of a farmer. In fact, although Martin's father, Hans Luther, came from solid peasant stock, he had gone to work as a miner and through hard work and persistence—traits he seems to have passed on to his eldest child—eventually became the owner of a smelter in the county of Mansfeld, where Martin was probably born in 1483. By the time Martin was about 10 years old, Hans was a respected member of the community and had been elected a municipal councilor. Mining was not always profitable, however, and young Martin was accustomed to a frugal household. His mother, Margarete, would often have to gather wood in the forest and bring it home to use as fuel.

Above, the devil delivers a declaration of war against Luther; at left, he carries off women accused of witchcraft who are being burned at the stake. To Luther and his contemporaries, Satan and witches, like sin and death, were real adversaries against whom eternal vigilance had to be maintained. During Luther's lifetime, four women who had been accused of witchcraft were executed in Wittenberg.

Both parents were devout and, like most of their neighbors, tended to incorporate elements of old German paganism into their Christian beliefs. For the Luthers, God was a stern judge, to be propitiated by the confession of sin and performance of penance and good deeds. The devil, just as real, was also present in the world, as were the elves, fairies, and witches who peopled the wind and the woods. Despite his later education, Luther never let go of these early beliefs, once declaring that "many regions are inhabited by devils."

From these modest, middle-class beginnings, Luther went off to the university at Erfurt in the summer of 1501. Located in central Germany, at the intersection of major trade routes, Erfurt lay in such a pretty spot that Luther called it a new Bethlehem. Between the city and the woods of the Thuringian Forest lay orchards, vineyards, and fields of brilliant flowers—flax, saffron, and the German indigo that supported the region's dye industry. From the midst of these colorful fields rose the city's seemingly impregnable walls and a skyline dominated by the towers of two large cathedrals. Indeed, Erfurt's ecclesiastical institutions were numerous, including 11 imposing churches belonging to monasteries of almost every order. These monasteries, along with parishes, artisan guilds, the city council, and the university, all took part in processions and celebrations, impressive in their multicolored banners, crosses, and candles.

Luther began his studies at the university in the faculty of liberal arts. After gaining his bachelor's degree, he would be able to enter one of the higher faculties, such as jurisprudence, medicine, or theology. Like all students, he had to live in one of the bursas, or residential colleges. Life in the bursa bore a striking resemblance to that in a monastery. Both were strictly regulated and supervised. In the bursa, students rose at 4:00 in the morning and went to bed at 8:00 in the evening. Living accommodations were spartan—large sleeping quarters and common study rooms—and meals were served twice a day, meat four times a week. Frivolity was frowned on and relations with the opposite sex strictly forbidden. Not surprisingly, some students thumbed their noses at these edicts, but Martin Luther was not one of them. Though he could be lively and convivial—at one point he learned to play the lute—he was also brooding and prone to a tormenting introspection and self-punishment in pursuit of spiritual grace.

As his father intended, Luther began law studies in 1505. But that July, on his way back to Erfurt from a visit home, he was caught in a sudden thunderstorm. Lightning struck nearby, knocking him to the ground. To Luther, steeped since childhood in the conviction that he had to answer to God, this was a direct experience of the presence of the Lord. "Help me, St. Anne, I will become a monk," Luther cried out to the saint who provided aid in times of danger from storms and sudden death.

Emerging unscathed, Luther kept his vow. Two weeks later, he presented himself as a novice to the Augustinian monastery, one of the few orders whose practices had lately been reformed and returned to rigor and austerity. When asked, he declared that he was ready to take on the burdens of the monastic life—the scant diet and rough clothing, the renunciation of self-will and the mortification of the flesh, the hardship of poverty and the shame of begging. Then his head was tonsured, leaving the crown bare, and his clothes exchanged for the habit of the novice.

Hans Luther, on learning the

A monk and a nun share a cup of wine in an intimate pose suggesting a betrayal of their vows of celibacy, which was not unknown among the religious orders of Luther's day. Priests sometimes lived openly with women in relationships akin to marriage, which the church punished by fining the straying clergy.

news, was beside himself with fury. Although he calmed down enough to be present when Martin performed his first Mass two years later, his anger burst out during the celebratory meal afterward, startling the other guests. "You learned scholar," Hans thundered, "have you never read in the Bible that you should honor your father and your mother? And here you have left me and your dear mother to look after ourselves in our old age." The son was taken aback but remained unshaken in his decision.

In 1511 Luther's order assigned him permanently to the University of Wittenberg. The following year he received his doctorate in theology and began to teach the Bible. The close reading of Scripture that he undertook at this point would have a profound impact on his thinking and beliefs. In the Epistle to the Romans, he came upon a sentence by Saint Paul: "The just shall live by faith." Luther had spent years wrestling with the question of his own salvation. Despite rigorous fasting, even to the point of endangering his health; incessant confession; and the performance of other forms of penance, he could never erase the doubt as to whether God forgave him his sins. But upon reading Paul's words, Martin felt his despair at being unworthy of salvation had been lifted. He found further sustenance in the writing of Saint Augustine, who had declared that the saved "are singled out not by their own merits, but by the grace of the Mediator; that is, they are justified . . . as by a free favour." The hope, courage, and certainty these words gave Luther set the course of action that would lead to his break with Rome.

In the year following his rancorous hearing with Cajetan in Augsburg, Luther's thinking and writing on the issues raised in his Ninety-five Theses deepened and expanded. Supporters rallied to Wittenberg and to Luther, whose warm and magnetic personality drew people to him. His penetrating baritone voice was a pleasure to listen to, and he never had to shout to be heard. Students flocked to his lectures, and when he began preaching to the monks in the tiny cloister church, the services had to be transferred to the larger town church (a separate and much older building than the castle church) to accommodate the crowd.

Among those who came under Luther's influence were theology professor Andreas Karlstadt and Philipp Melanchthon, a young prodigy and professor of Greek, who agreed with Luther's interpretation of the words of Saint Paul. Although Luther would break with Karlstadt within a few years, Melanchthon would remain a close and valued confidant for the rest of his life. "Never was there a greater man on the face of the earth," Melanchthon once wrote of Luther. "I would rather die than separate myself from this man." And of course, one of Luther's staunchest allies was Georg Spalatin, Frederick's secretary and chaplain. Indeed, Spalatin's adroit mediation and timely interventions would be credited with Luther's survival in the face of threats from both the papacy and the empire.

Restive imperial knights such as Ulrich von Hutten and Franz von Sickingen also rallied to the Wittenberg professor. The knights, and Hutten in particular, tended to give Luther's opposition to Rome a patriotic meaning. For them it represented a fight to free the German states from foreign influence.

In a debate at Leipzig in July, Luther argued with Johann Eck, a Dominican friar and professor at the University of Ingolstadt, against the primacy of the pope and his office in Rome as being of divine origin, pointing out that in the early centuries of Christianity, bishops outside of Rome were neither confirmed by nor subject to Rome. The Greek bishops, for example, never acknowledged the Roman pope's primacy. Luther's statements challenged the entire hierarchy of the Roman Catholic Church.

Despite these direct attacks on its authority, Rome remained remarkably quiet at first, its attention diverted by the death in January 1519 of Emperor Maximilian I. The pope became primarily concerned with manipulating the election of an imperial successor. Luther made good use of the lull. He kept preaching about his ideas and publishing treatises explaining his positions and responding to those of his critics. In early 1519, a printer in Basel, Switzerland, brought out a single edition that included the Ninety-five Theses and the subsequent Resolutions, explaining and refining the original points.

Luther's work was in great demand. The theologian's revolutionary ideas were conveyed in a rich, forceful German, filled with catchy proverbs and earthy phrases. He created striking images and stirred powerful feelings. Printers snapped up everything he wrote. It was not unusual to see a printer's apprentice, armed with page proofs for Luther's latest publication, racing through the streets of Wittenberg to the Black Cloister, where he would wait impatiently for Luther to review them before rushing back to the press with the corrections. Fortunately, Luther was a prolific

which Luther himself was never present, Rome issued the papal bull *Exsurge Domine* in June 1520. Luther had 60 days (from the day the bull was actually received by him) to recant erroneous and heretical statements or face excommunication. In the meantime, his books were to be burned.

At this point, the logistical realities of the slow pace of 16th-century communications conspired with the political realities of the delicate relationship between church and empire to buy Luther more time. First two papal nuncios were dispatched to get the bull published in central Germany and other parts of the empire. This entailed not only getting it reprinted but also persuading the secular authorities to cooperate in its dissemination.

Only in three places—one of which was Brandenburg, Saxony's longtime rival—did the nuncio succeed in having the bull officially posted.

"The dam has broken, and I cannot stem the waters."

writer, who was capable of producing 20 to 30 works a year.

Most publications were in pamphlet form, six or eight pages that could be sold cheaply and thus received wide distribution. A publisher in Basel, a bastion of printing, wrote Luther that 600 copies of his books had been sent to France and Spain, while many others had gone with a bookseller to Italy. "We have sold out all your books except ten copies, and never remember to have sold any more quickly." Luther received a letter from a former classmate who reported that followers in Rome—at great risk to their lives—were distributing the Reformer's tracts practically beneath the Vatican's nose.

By January 1520, the question of Luther had become too pressing for further delay, and the Vatican began new proceedings against the monk. After considerable deliberation, during

In many other places, the bulk of the common people were on Luther's side, and authorities either were afraid to oppose the popular tide or were in sympathy with it. Even a number of bishops were reluctant and held off publishing the bull for as long as six months. The duke of Bavaria feared that publication of the bull would start riots. Indeed, in Erfurt, where the papal nuncio did manage to have copies of the bull printed, students at Luther's alma mater christened it a "bulloon"—and threw the copies in the river to see whether they would float. Supporters began making the case to the emperor that Luther had never been given a fair hearing, before a properly appointed court.

The bull took three months to reach Luther. Meanwhile, Luther continued to publish. In August, *An Address to the German Nobility* spelled out a comprehensive program of reform in

which, among other things, he asked the emperor and secular princes to protect their citizens against ecclesiastical interference and extortion. The church, Luther declared, should renounce its temporal possessions and claims, and its income—annates, indulgences, crusading taxes, and various other fees—should be eliminated. The clergy should be allowed to marry, the number of religious orders reduced, and there should be no irrevocable vows taken. There should be no papal primacy in the interpretation of Scripture. Simmering beneath it all was a burning indignation at church corruption. Luther repeatedly compared the pope's pomp and circumstance with the humility of Christ.

In September, the Reformer produced his most radical publication to date: *A Prelude*

In a printer's workshop, three compositors set type *(left)* and another man inks it *(rear)*, while a fellow worker operates one of two presses *(right)*. A young apprentice stacks the printed pages on a central table. Invented around 1440, movable lead type allowed for mass production of reading material; by 1500 more than 200 European cities had presses.

concerning the Babylonian Captivity of the Church. In a stroke he eliminated confirmation, marriage, ordination, and extreme unction as sacraments, religious rites through which grace was conferred on the faithful by the select few, namely, priests. He based this elimination on the grounds that these four rites were nowhere explicitly described in the New Testament and thus were not sacraments directly instituted by Christ. Rather, through historical development, the church had made them such for its own purposes. He reserved as sacraments only baptism, Communion, and an evangelical form of penance. It was a radical notion that challenged the centuries-old doctrinal authority of the pope.

The papal bull finally reached Luther in Wittenberg on the 10th of October, the same month Maximilian's 19-year-old grandson, Charles I of Spain, was crowned Emperor Charles V. By now the monk had fully realized and accepted the finality of his break with Rome. If papal law condemned him, he was prepared to condemn it in turn. In October and November, Luther got word that his books had been burned in Louvain, Liège, and Cologne, albeit not without opposition. In response he arranged for a conflagration of his own. On December 10, Philipp Melanchthon issued an invitation to the students and faculty of the university to a bonfire. At ten that evening, works of scholastic theology and canon law—which had influenced secular laws throughout medieval Europe—would be cast into the flames.

At the appointed hour, the pyre was ignited. As the flames roared higher, students and theologians who supported Luther crowded round to throw several editions of canon law on the fire, followed by some of the writings of Luther's enemies. Then Luther appeared, trembling, the papal bull in his hands. Standing as near the roaring fire as he dared, he began to speak, his words reminiscent of the 21st Psalm: "Because you have confounded the truth of God, today the Lord confounds you. Into the fire with you!" With that, he cast the papal bull into the inferno and

Challenging the Catholic belief that baptism is a sacrament only priests can perform, layman and Luther supporter Philipp Melanchthon baptizes a baby *(above).* At right, Luther and his followers toss the papal bull threatening him with excommunication along with books of church law into a bonfire in Wittenberg. The event was defiantly publicized by Melanchthon, author of the first systematic statement of the Lutheran faith. "This little Greek," Luther wrote fondly of the gifted Wittenberg professor, "surpasses me even in theology itself."

stepped back. Afterward, the students paraded through town with another copy of the bull stuck on a pole and an indulgence on the point of a sword.

Frederick the Wise, in his boldest declaration yet, wrote to the imperial court to excuse Luther's act. He noted that Luther's books had been burned despite the monk's repeated assertion that he was ready to do "everything consistent with the name of Christian." Frederick also pointed out that he himself had constantly requested that Luther not be "condemned unheard, nor should his books be burned." Finally, the elector added, "If now

he has given tit for tat, I hope that His Imperial Majesty will graciously overlook it."

After Luther's failure to recant, Rome officially excommunicated him in January 1521. What would the new emperor, a self-confessed defender of the faith, do? Left to his own devices, Charles, who had promised on his life to protect the church and the honor of the pope, probably would have followed Rome's lead swiftly. However, he also had an imperial constitution to obey, one clause of which stipulated that no German should be taken for trial outside Germany, another that no German should

be outlawed without a hearing. In the end, after a considerable amount of back and forth, Martin Luther was invited to make his case in April 1521 at the Diet of Worms.

The imperial diet, or general assembly, had been convened in the southwestern city of Worms in January. Though it took place on German soil and primarily concerned the German states, it was an international affair as well, attended by the Spanish, the Italians, the French, and the English. Various constitutional questions as well as the voting of monies to finance Charles's journey to Rome for his official coronation were addressed. The Germans also put forth their *Grievances of the German Nation against Rome,* in which they complained about Roman exploitation, including the selling of indulgences.

Their grievances were part and parcel of the question of Luther. Some of the laity interpreted Luther's religious themes as defenses of local autonomy and the customary law of Germany against papal jurisdiction, winning Luther a lot more backing than a purely spiritual interpretation of his teaching would have brought. Clearly, support for Luther included a large dose of anti-Roman sentiment, and many of the Reformer's compatriots regarded him as the very embodiment of the German people.

Luther's journey from Wittenberg to Worms, in contrast to the one he had made to Augsburg three years earlier, seemed like a triumphal parade. Led by the imperial herald and traveling with several colleagues in a carriage drawn by three horses, Luther was met and surrounded by jubilant throngs everywhere. "All of Germany is in an utter uproar," the papal nuncio Aleander had reported to Rome earlier in the year. "Nine-tenths of the people are shouting 'Luther,' and the other tenth—if Luther is of no consequence to them—at least have 'Death to the Roman court!' as their slogan."

By now Luther's youthful emaciation had given way to a certain incipient stoutness, but his deep-set eyes still burned with

passion and his fiery sermons lit up the crowds everywhere he preached en route to Worms. Those who had until then only read his work had their admiration of the man confirmed. In Erfurt, where his party was escorted into the city by 40 horsemen, his sermon drew so many listeners that the balcony of the church where he spoke began to creak.

Despite numerous warnings that the emperor had reneged on his promise of safe-conduct and the urging of several of his supporters not to continue into the lion's den at Worms, Luther persisted, arriving outside the city at ten in the morning on April 16. A party of 100 horsemen came out to escort him, only to discover such a crush of people inside the gates that they could barely enter. Thousands of spectators filled the streets, hung out of windows, and perched in the branches of trees. At the door to the hostel where Luther would be lodged, a monk knelt to touch the hem of the Reformer's robe, as if he were a saint. Luther looked at the crowd and said simply, "God will be with me," then he turned and went inside.

Luther's appearance before the imperial diet began on the late afternoon of April 17. The imperial councilors had decided that the monk would be asked just two questions: Did he acknowledge authorship of his books, and was he prepared to recant them in whole or in part? Luther, who had once again, as at Augsburg, been expecting a real hearing, seemed taken aback and asked in a subdued voice to be given a day to formulate his response.

The next night, in flickering torchlight in a packed hall, Luther delivered his answer to the diet in a 10-minute speech in German, which he later repeated in Latin. Translators were kept busy as Charles V, like many others present, spoke neither German nor Latin. Speaking loudly and fearlessly, Luther stood by all his writings. Some stated simple Christian truths, ones that even some of his opponents acknowledged; to recant those truths was unthinkable. Some books criticized the actions of the papacy and

A War of Words and Images

After the invention of the printing press in the 15th century, the Catholic Church created the first wave of mass-produced printed material—letters of indulgence. Protestants struck back in the 1520s and 1530s, flooding Europe with pamphlets, sermons, and books in support of the Reformation. In 1523 alone, nearly 500 new titles were published (about one-third of them by Luther), all but 80 of which dealt with the Reformation. By midcentury, some 10,000 different Protestant titles had been printed and disseminated.

Two common themes of reform propaganda were the true church versus the false church and Christ versus the Antichrist, with the latter usually portrayed as the pope. There were also virulent attacks on abuses of monasticism, with pamphleteers portraying monks and nuns as parasites on society who indulged in gluttony, drunkenness, sexual immorality, and other despicable acts. One writer dismissed monastic orders as "plunderers of bodies, souls, honor, and goods" and referred to the pope

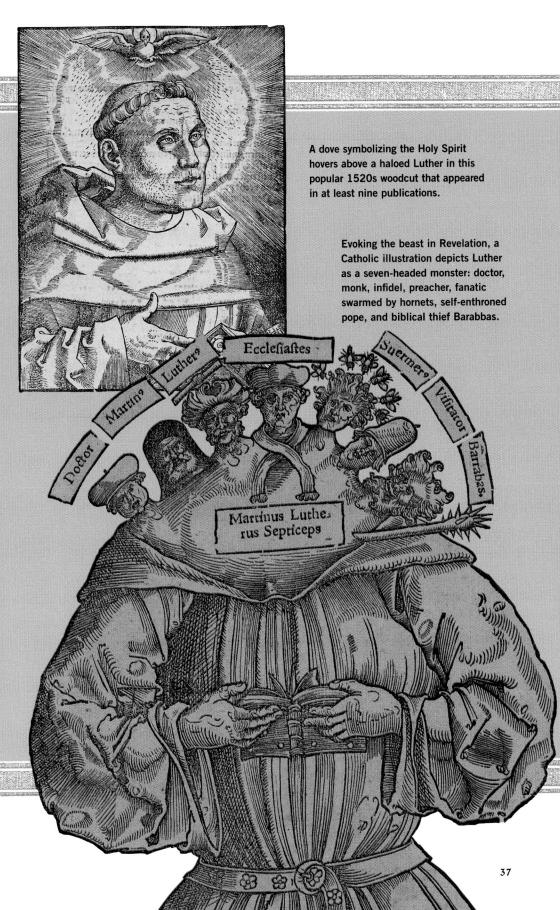

A dove symbolizing the Holy Spirit hovers above a haloed Luther in this popular 1520s woodcut that appeared in at least nine publications.

Evoking the beast in Revelation, a Catholic illustration depicts Luther as a seven-headed monster: doctor, monk, infidel, preacher, fanatic swarmed by hornets, self-enthroned pope, and biblical thief Barabbas.

37

as the "great raging Babylonian whore."

Pamphleteers heaped scorn on the laity for being too gullible and accepting pronouncements of the church out of fear. As one-time Franciscan Heinrich von Kettenbach wrote: "Faced with death, people are easily drawn into superstition and gross idolatry. No one truly trusts in Jesus Christ for his salvation."

Writers expected their pamphlets, most of which were 20 pages or less in length, to be read aloud at gatherings, since only a small percentage of the total population could read. Ideas were also conveyed by pictures, and most publications were illustrated with woodcuts. "Without images,"

Luther wrote, "we can neither think nor understand anything." In 1521 Lucas Cranach produced 26 woodcuts comparing the pope unfavorably with Jesus. They appeared in a small booklet entitled *Passional Christi und Antichristi* with commentary by Wittenberg professor and Luther ally Philipp Melanchthon.

The Protestant publications reflected the hope for a more biblical church and a more just society. Writers tried to send the message that the laity had a right to study and interpret the Scripture for themselves. As one author noted, "We, the sheep, also have the right to judge the doctrine and preaching of our shepherds."

In a clever cartoon of a cardinal, the artist reveals his opinion of the clergyman's true nature; when the picture is turned upside down, he becomes a fool.

In two scenes from Lucas Cranach and Philipp Melanchthon's popular *Passional Christi und Antichristi*, the lives of Jesus Christ and the pope are contrasted. On the left, in a scene from the Bible, Jesus washes his disciples' feet, while on the right, kings kiss the feet of the pope.

the Roman Curia, which helped the pope govern and administer the church, and some condemned canonical laws. To refute them would be to strengthen tyranny and open the doors to godlessness. "Good God, what sort of tool of evil and tyranny I then would be!" exclaimed Luther. Above the council, above the pope, stood the Holy Scripture. If, he declared, his writings could be refuted by biblical evidence, he would be willing to throw any of his books into the fire himself.

But the imperial diet did not intend to enter into a disputation with him. Instead, the councilors asked Luther to make an unequivocal reply to the question of his heretical statements.

Luther answered, voice firm and clear, "Unless I am convinced by the testimony of the Scriptures or by clear reason (for I do not trust either in the pope or in councils alone, since it is well known that they have often erred and contradicted themselves), I am bound by the Scriptures I have quoted and my conscience is captive to the Word of God. I cannot and I will not retract anything, since it is neither safe nor right to go against conscience. May God help me. Amen."

The hall erupted in noise, one of the councilors began to argue with Luther, and an angry emperor jumped to his feet and stormed out of the room. As the meeting broke up, the jeering and hissing Spaniards in the crowd shouted, "To the fire with him!" But outside, surrounded by friends, Luther shouted triumphantly in turn, "I am through; I am through!"

On the 19th of April, Charles summoned

This horrific beast's batlike wings brand it as being in league with the devil, while its distorted three-tiered crown and cross-embroidered slippers clearly show that it is meant to be a depiction of the pope.

39

the German princes. The emperor, grayish blue eyes alight in his harsh young face, contemplated the assembly before he spoke. He reminded them of the fate of the condemned heretic Jan Hus in Konstanz. "I am determined to hold fast by all which has happened since the Council of Konstanz. It is certain that a single monk must err if he stands against the opinion of all Christendom. . . . Therefore I am determined to set my kingdoms and dominions, my friends, my body, my blood, my life, my soul upon it," the emperor vowed. "From now on I regard [Luther] as a notorious heretic."

Despite the danger, people flocked to Luther to offer their support, among them nobles and knights, impressed that a German had faced the foreigners who came to Germany to rule. Placards clearly supporting Luther appeared in Worms. One read, "Bundschuh! Bundschuh! Bundschuh!" the term for a peasant's leather shoe and the symbol of the rebellious peasants. Another mocked the youth of the emperor: "Woe to the land whose king is a child."

Charles would not be intimidated. He promised that he would honor a safe-conduct for Luther's return to Wittenberg, but after that, authorities would be empowered to move against him. A proviso to the safe-conduct forbade Luther to preach on his journey home. On April 26, Luther and a few companions left Worms for Wittenberg. The Reformer never reached his destination.

Slowly the story of Luther's fate came to light. Within days of leaving Worms, he had broken the terms of the imperial safe-conduct, preaching in two villages along his route home. On the day following the second sermon, May 4, he, two companions, and a driver for their wagon followed the road northward as it wound through the Thuringian Forest. Suddenly, armed horsemen broke from the trees. One of Luther's party immediately jumped from the wagon and fled, but further escape was prevented when the attackers knocked the driver from the wagon with a violent blow and aimed their crossbows at Luther and his remaining companion. The horsemen demanded the travelers' names. When Luther gave his, he was dragged from the wagon and forced to run alongside the horsemen as they rode into the trees and disappeared from sight. When Luther's traveling companions reached safety and told their awful tale, the news spread across Europe. Many people were certain the Reformer had been killed. The German artist Albrecht Dürer wrote in his diary, "O God, if Luther is dead, who now will teach us the holy Gospel so clearly?"

But one member of Luther's party, his trusted friend Nikolaus von Amsdorf, had every reason to believe the religious leader was alive and well. When the abductors had come crashing through the trees, Luther had leaned over and whispered to Amsdorf: "Do not become excited. We are among friends."

Though he had not been told the details, Luther had known before he left Worms that a secret plan had been hatched to whisk him away to safety. Frederick had been the instigator, but even he was not to know the method by which the monk was to be abducted or where he would be taken. This would allow the elector to plead ignorance if questioned about the matter, thus protecting him from action by the church. As one contemporary later wrote, "Many people at the diet also believed that it was a real captivity, so well was the secret kept."

Luther's abductors had taken him to one of Frederick's own castles, the Wartburg, a nearly uninhabited fortress not far from Eisenach, where Luther had last preached. There he was told to stay in his rooms until both his tonsure and beard grew out, helping him to maintain the disguise he would take on for the next 10 months—that of a Junker, or knight, by the name of Jörg. Most of those who maintained the Wartburg were kept in ignorance of the Junker's true identity.

Junker Jörg appeared to be one of the imperial knights, a minor aristocracy whose titles had been granted by the Holy Roman emperor. They had fallen on hard times, their economic and political role fading. Many were forced against their wishes to take service with the Catholic Church. Dissatisfaction made many supportive of reform.

Ulrich von Hutten, who had entered the service of the archbishop–elector of Mainz in 1517, painted a fairly bleak picture of his own circumstances in angry response to someone who had suggested he leave court service and return to his castle. "You city people, who lead comfortable, placid, easygoing lives, seem to think that a man in my position can find peace and quiet in his country retreat. Are you so ignorant of the turmoil and insecurity to which my sort is subject?"

Hutten went on to enumerate the difficulties of a knight. "Our days are spent in the fields, in the woods, and in fortified strongholds. We lease our land to a few starveling

In the Wittenberg church, Martin Luther delivers a sermon to a spellbound congregation. The Augustinian monk initially stepped into the pulpit with great humility, having been chosen by the city council to preach in the church "against my will." He proved to be among the age's most powerful preachers.

peasants who barely manage to scratch a living from it. From such paupers we draw our revenues, an income hardly worth the labor spent on it." Furthermore, he said, most knights were dependent on a prince "to whom our hope of safety is attached" and even that safety was not certain. "If I fall into the hands of those who are at war with my overlord, they seize me and . . . if my luck is bad I lose half my patrimony in ransom." As a consequence, Hutten said, "I cannot travel a mile from my home without putting on armor."

As for "home," Hutten could boast few comforts in the stone castles the knights built for defense. "Girded by moats and walls, they are narrow and crowded inside, pigs and cows competing with men for space, dark rooms crammed with guns, pitch, sulfur, and other materials of war. The stench of gunpowder hangs in the air mixed with the smell of dogs and excrement and other such pleasant odors. Knights and retainers go to and fro, among them thieves and highway robbers, for our houses are open to all, and how can we tell one armed man from another?"

The knight lived far from the bustle of the city, but "peace and quiet" were nowhere to be found. "There is a constant din of sheep bleating, cows lowing, dogs barking, men working in the fields, and the squeaks and creakings of carts and wagons. Wolves can be heard howling in the woods beyond the fields."

While Hutten's castle may have been a noisy and noisome source of worry and anxiety to him, the Wartburg proved for Martin Luther, whose residence was temporary, a place he could catch his breath after the confrontation at Worms. He took long walks through the woods and fields. On one occasion, he was taken along on a hunt, but he proved a poor hunter. As he later wrote, "With great pains I saved a little live rabbit, and rolled it up in the sleeve of my cloak." But when he let the rabbit go where he thought it would be safe, the dogs sniffed it out and pounced. "Thus," he noted, "do the Pope and Satan rage to kill souls and are not stopped by my labor."

Luther devoted most of his time at the Wartburg to writing and was incredibly productive, finishing, among other things, a translation of the New Testament into German. But worrying reports reached him that supporters in Wittenberg were moving reform along far too quickly. Andreas Karlstadt, for example, who had been arousing the laity with his sermons and publications, announced on December 22 that he would celebrate a simple evangelical Lord's Supper on New Year's Day at the castle church. When the elector's counselors sought to stop this event, Karlstadt moved it up.

On Christmas Day 1521, Karlstadt conducted a service in which he did not wear the Mass vestments. The participants took Communion without having previously fasted or gone to confession, and Karlstadt, giving his sermon in German, encouraged the laity to come to the altar, help themselves to the bread, and take the chalice into their own hands. In the process, bread—the Host—was dropped, terrifying the man who had been holding it. Duke George of Albertine Saxony complained to the emperor and other members of the Diet at Nürnberg of having heard that "the blood of our Lord is served not in a chalice but in a mug."

Disturbances and vandalism of churches erupted. Images and altars were forcibly removed and destroyed. "The dam has broken," Philipp Melanchthon said, "and I cannot stem the waters." When word of the violent upheavals got back to Luther, he felt compelled to return from exile. In doing so, he was once again putting his life in jeopardy. Back in May, Emperor Charles V had gotten an edict passed that placed Luther under the imperial ban. All imperial citizens were forbidden to have dealings with the monk; in fact, each had a duty to seize Luther and turn him over to the imperial authorities if possible. Failing that, he could be killed on sight.

The prospect of Luther's reappearance worried Fred-

Pictured at right is Wartburg, the castle that served as a refuge for Martin Luther in his disguise as a knight, following the Diet of Worms. Yet while his physical safety was assured, his spiritual struggles raged on, for "in this idle solitude," he wrote to a companion, "there are a thousand battles with Satan."

erick, who had somehow persuaded the emperor to exempt him from having to serve Luther the imperial ban in Saxony and who now feared the consequences if Luther was to return to public life. Luther wrote the elector that his, Luther's, safety was less important than restoring order to the church and community in Wittenberg. Frederick should simply let events unfold, Luther said, and explicitly absolved his patron of any responsibility if the empire took action or even took his life. "If I thought your Grace could and would defend me by force, I should not come. The sword ought not and cannot decide a matter of this kind."

Traveling in his disguise as Junker Jörg, Luther made his way back to Wittenberg in March 1522. The journey was more dangerous than even those to Augsburg and Worms, for now he was under both the papal and imperial ban and could count on protection from no quarter. One night during a severe storm, a pair of Swiss travelers came upon him in a village inn. Noticing that this knight, wrapped in a scarlet cloak, was reading a book in Hebrew, they asked if he knew if Luther was in Wittenberg. "I know quite positively that he is not," the knight replied, "but he will be."

Upon reaching Wittenberg, Luther began a series of eight sermons in which, in his steady, soothing voice, he stressed that the Christian cannot resort to force but must rely on the power of the Word alone to achieve reform. "I will preach it, teach it, write it, but I will constrain no man by force, for faith must come freely without compulsion."

Not all of the protests were violent. Some protesters used mockery to undermine the church. Elaborate parodies of solemn church rituals were acted out, on one occasion using animal bones to represent a bishop's relics and flying rags as ceremonial flags. Indulgences were used to make carnival costumes or as toilet paper.

But the violent acts of those who smashed images and threatened priests were a greater source of pain to Luther than anything he had suffered at the hands of Rome.

Knight, poet laureate of Germany, and humanist Ulrich von Hutten was one of the first nationalists to demand German political freedom from Rome. Having first dismissed Luther's controversy as a squabble among monks, he came to champion Luther's cause, thinking it a way to gain freedom for Germany. Hutten hoped that Emperor Charles V would rid Germany of Roman interference and was severely disappointed when the emperor banned Luther instead.

Consequently, Hutten was unable to secure a permanent position with any ruler. After his only ally against the princes and priests was killed in a petty war in May 1523, Hutten fled to Basel, Switzerland, where he sought help from his old friend Erasmus. But because he had recently denounced Erasmus for not supporting Luther, Erasmus turned him away. Hutten then tried to blackmail the humanist, threatening to publish a pamphlet attacking him. But that plan also failed and the knight was driven out of Basel and other towns before taking refuge on an island in Lake Zürich. There, exiled and ill, the once distinguished author wrote with his dying breath, "I do not give up hope that a time will come when God will once again gather together the men of courage who are now dispersed."

Luther's appeals restored reason. Karlstadt took over a congregation in a neighboring town, and another preacher, Gabriel Zwilling, agreed to give up celebrating Communion wearing feathers in his beret. The public peace of Wittenberg returned.

In addition to its threats to Luther's life, the emperor's Edict of Worms prohibited the copying, printing, and sale of Luther's writings as well as their reading, possession, and preaching. Despite these prohibitions, the evangelical movement developed in comparative security, largely due to the independence of the German princes and imperial free cities. Luther's books continued to be printed and sold quite openly in the German states. By contrast, the ban was strictly enforced in the Netherlands and Spain, countries under the emperor's direct control.

The new theology thus was soon spread throughout much of northern Europe, thanks to Wittenberg-trained preachers who were appointed to serve in many cities and small towns. Between 1520 and 1560, more than a third of the 176 evangelical preachers in Germany had studied at the University of Wittenberg. These men carried out the work of the new theology by preaching in the vernacular, reading the Bible aloud, and conducting catechism practice. Thus, even though much of the Reformation's effect was disseminated through books and pamphlets—"Printing is God's latest and best work to spread the true religion throughout the world," Luther once said—the real work of conversion took place through the spoken word. There was Guillaume Farel in Switzerland and Leonhard Stöckel in Hungary. In Scandinavia, where Luther's Reformation made the biggest impact outside Germany, Hans Tausen spread the message in Denmark and Olaus Petri took it to Sweden; both had studied at Wittenberg. Traveling preacher Thomas Müntzer, far more radical than Luther, was expelled from several places—Allstedt, Mühlhausen, Prague—as the extreme views he had developed caused him to lose the goodwill of both the ecclesiastical and civic authorities.

Perhaps the most dramatic and dangerous work that Luther himself undertook in these years was that of aiding monks and nuns who wished to leave the cloister. In *On Monastic Vows,* published in 1521, Luther had declared the monk's vow to be not founded in Scripture, resting on the false assumption that superior Christians have a special calling, or vocation, to strive for perfection. In fact, said Luther, there is no special religious vocation; rather, God calls each man as he is engaged in ordinary tasks. "This is the work," one observer commented, "which emptied the cloisters." The Wittenberg Augustinians, for example, more or less dissolved themselves, abandoning the

Black Cloister and leaving Luther to live in it alone for a while.

In most of the reformed cities, however, members of monastic orders were given the choice of adopting the new theology or being exiled. In some towns, mendicant friars, who seemed most resistant to the Reformation, were thrown out of their houses by destructive mobs. But as townspeople came to realize that many monks and nuns had no secular vocational skills or place to go, a cloister for monks and for nuns would often be allowed to continue in existence while being forbidden to recruit new members, thereby allowing older monks and nuns to live out their lives unmolested. Whether voluntarily, by fiat, or by attrition, a whole class of people in Europe who were once considered special lost their "holiness."

In challenging the celibate ideal Luther extolled marriage as the better state, especially in light of centuries of clerical sexual hypocrisy. Not only did priests take mates and father children, but the church had profited from human desire by collecting annual penitential fees from such clergy. Priests should be free to marry, Luther said, if only to end this false chastity. Moreover, marriage was good for society. It created sound bodies, clear consciences, and strong families. Marriage was the foundation of household order, just as families were the basis of society at large.

When nuns in a village across the border in Albertine Saxony, the territory of Duke George, asked Luther's advice on leaving the cloister, Luther arranged it. Since this would be in open violation of both canon and civil law, the escape had to be well planned and highly secret. Duke George, an implacable foe of the Reformation, had already executed a man who had done what the Reformer intended. Luther found help from a respected elderly merchant, Leonhard Koppe of Torgau, who delivered barrels of herring to the convent in question and whose own daughter was a nun there. Evidently, Koppe hid 12 frightened and excited nuns in his covered wagon as if they were empty herring barrels and brought them out to safety. He deposited three

with their families in electoral Saxony and took nine whose homes were in Albertine Saxony to Wittenberg. Luther later praised Koppe's effort as an example to all parents whose children were in cloisters, comparing it to the deliverance of the children of Israel from Egyptian bondage.

"A wagon load of vestal virgins has just come to town," one Wittenberg student wrote to a friend, "all the more eager for marriage than for life. God grant them husbands lest worse befall." Luther did manage to find them all husbands, or at least homes or positions of some sort. Among the nuns was 24-year-old Katherine von Bora, whose father had placed her in a nunnery when she was about 10. She took her vows at age 16. At one point after the escape from the convent, Bora fell in love with and thought she would marry a former Wittenberg student. But the student's patrician family in Nürnberg apparently objected to their son's marrying a runaway nun, and the wedding never took place.

Luther then tried to marry her off to an unpopular pastor with the reputation for miserliness. Bora, a proud and independent sort, refused him. She let Luther know that she would, however, consider marrying him or his friend Amsdorf. Luther was taken aback; for the last few years, his friends had been suggesting he should marry, but he had not taken them seriously. As he wrote to one: "[I] am not now inclined to take a wife. Not that I lack the feelings of a man . . . , but my mind is averse to marriage because I daily expect the death decreed to the heretic." But after discussing the situation with his parents—who urged him to marry and carry on the family name—Luther agreed to wed Katherine himself.

Martin Luther, age 42, was legally betrothed and wed to Katherine von Bora, age 26, on Tuesday, June 13, 1525. The ceremony took place in the Black Cloister, where Martin was already residing. It was a private ceremony, attended only by a few friends, among them Lucas Cranach, who was Luther's best man.

(Bora had been staying at Cranach's house, where Luther had been a frequent visitor.)

In many ways, the wedding went against tradition—and not only because of the former occupations of the bride and groom. While Tuesday was the customary day of the week for a wedding, it was not customary to become betrothed and wed on the same day. Weddings were usually public events, with a large number of the local citizenry participating. There was commonly a public procession to the church, where the ceremony was usually performed either outside the front doors or inside.

The Luthers did follow the tradition of having witnesses accompany them into their bedroom, where the couple symbolically lay down on the marriage bed. A small meal followed, enlivened by Franconian wine provided for the occasion by the town council, to which Lucas Cranach had been elected in 1522.

The new husband later explained the abbreviated engagement ceremony: "It is very dangerous to put off your wedding, for Satan gladly interferes and makes great trouble through evil talkers, slanderers, and friends." Indeed Martin Luther's opponents quickly spread rumors that he had married Katherine only after "dishonoring her" by having sex with her before their marriage. Even friends wondered and condemned the secrecy or spoke disparagingly about Katherine. Hoping to rectify the situation, the Luthers sent invitations for a special wedding celebration on June 27 to family and friends. Martin sent one to his longtime ally and friend Georg Spalatin. "You must come to my wedding. I have made the angels laugh and the devils weep." Leonhard Koppe, who had spirited Katherine and her fellow nuns out of the convent, was invited to leave his herrings behind but bring a keg of

though he did receive a small honorarium from the city government for preaching services. Much of his money had gone to supporting runaway monks and nuns, who were ill prepared to earn a living in the outside world. Luther considered charging tuition for his lectureship, a practice unknown in Wittenberg. Fortunately, Frederick the Wise's successor, his brother John, established a salary, to be paid from the elector's own pocket, to compensate Luther for his university duties. John also saw that Luther received compensation in food, clothing fabric, firewood, and household goods.

Martin was improvident and blithe about financial matters, although he helped Katherine take care of a garden that kept the family supplied with lettuce, peas, melons, beans, cucumbers, and cabbage. It was thanks to his wife, whom he affectionately called Katie, that the fam-

"You must come to my wedding. I have made the angels laugh and the devils weep."

"the best Torgau beer" to the feast. Katherine and Martin kept the celebration to one day, in accordance with city ordinances.

The Luthers set up housekeeping in the Black Cloister. The second floor was converted into living quarters. For a man long accustomed to the monk's life, marriage took some getting used to. On the one hand, Luther appreciated having his bed made and his laundry washed: "Before I was married the bed was not made for a whole year and became foul with sweat. But I worked so hard and was so weary I tumbled in without noticing." On the other hand, there was another person now to take into account: "One wakes up in the morning and finds a pair of pigtails on the pillow which were not there before."

Martin Luther started out married life in bad financial straits. He had always refused to accept money for his writings,

ily could make ends meet. Katie managed the care of not only the house—which would eventually include several children—but also an orchard that gave peaches, apples, pears, grapes, and nuts and a fishpond that supplied perch, carp, trout, and pike. She even slaughtered the necessary fowl, pigs, and cows.

Katherine Luther became an astute businesswoman. She remodeled the cloister so she could take in as many as 30 student boarders. Quarters in the Black Cloister proved popular, since it offered close association with the great Reformer. She also repaired the cloister brewery, and her beer became so renowned that Martin once took samples to John's court. Her skill as an herbalist and her mastery of poultices and massage were also widely regarded in the community. One of her sons, who later became a doctor, considered his mother almost a doctor herself.

"Do Not Belch or Cry Out"

In 16th-century Europe, it was the duty of both parents to raise their children, with women playing the major role during a child's first years and men becoming increasingly involved after age six. But many observers accused parents of not teaching proper manners to their children. One pastor admonished parents who allowed their offspring to "creep about idly, eating and drinking whenever they please." Recognizing the need for instruction in this area, shoemaker and composer Hans Sachs published the guide below.

Listen you children who are going to table.
Wash your hands and cut your nails.
Do not sit at the head of the table;
This is reserved for the father of the house.
Do not commence eating until a blessing is
    said.
Dine in God's name.
And permit the eldest to begin first.
Proceed in a disciplined manner.
Do not snort or smack like a pig.
Do not reach violently for bread,
Lest you may knock over a glass.
Do not cut bread on your chest,
Or conceal pieces of bread or pastry under
    your hands.
Do not tear pieces for your plate with your
    teeth.
Do not stir food around in your plate

Or linger over it.
Rushing through your meal is bad manners.
Do not reach for more food
While your mouth is still full,
Nor talk with your mouth full . . .
Do not belch or cry out.
With drink be most prudent . . .
Do not toast a person a second time.
Do not stare at a person
As if you were watching him eat.
Do not elbow the person sitting next to you.
Sit up straight; be a model of gracefulness.
Do not rock back and forth on the bench,
Lest you let loose a stink.
Do not kick your feet under the table.
Guard yourself against all shameful
Words, gossip, ridicule, and laughter
And be honorable in all matters.

If sexual play occurs at table,
Pretend you do not see it. . . .
Never scratch your head
(This goes for girls and women too),
Or fish out lice.
Let no one wipe his mouth on the table cloth,
Or lay his head in his hands.
Do not lean back against the wall
Until the meal is finished.
Silently praise and thank God
For the food he has graciously provided
And you have received from his fatherly
    hand.
Now you rise from the table,
Wash your hands,
And return diligently to your business or
    work.
Thus sayeth Hans Sachs, shoemaker.

However, it was Katherine's beer, not her herbs, that her insomniac husband imbibed to help him sleep.

Katherine Luther's myriad enterprises were not unusual for women at the time. Artisans' wives not only worked alongside their husbands but also performed wage labor for others. Although regulated by city councils, which had to placate men's guilds that did not want competition from women, butchers' and bakers' wives were often allowed to maintain the business when their husbands died, and especially needy women were allowed to bake and sell cakes, pretzels, and cookies. Women worked as maids in other households as well as doing day labor, such as washing or cooking. For many women such service was a stage of life, lasting until they were old enough to marry and had accumulated a small dowry; for other women, whose husbands had died and left them penniless, it was the only means of support. And for still other women, who worked their way up in a large household, the work became a permanent career.

People in domestic service were such a large and shifting population that some cities set up systems of employment agents to see to their regulation. Although both men and women were employment agents in the 15th century, by the 16th century, the occupation was strictly for women. They were required to hang out a shingle in front of their homes so that young boys and girls coming in from the countryside to look for work could find them. The agents were expected to send would-be servants to rich and modest households alike, but not to those who were known to mistreat their employees.

In the crafts, women's guilds of silkmakers and gold spinners emerged in Cologne and Zürich. In Nürnberg, Frankfurt, Munich, and Strasbourg, women were allowed to run their own breweries. The daughters of merchants were often taught to

Shoes are crafted in a busy shop while the shoemaker's wife waits on customers. As "bone of his bone," a wife was expected to be a partner, not a servant, to her husband in the family business and at home. Like the sun and the moon, husband and wife had their rightful and respected places.

keep the books in their fathers' businesses, and merchants' wives took over the business if their husbands died. Capable widows managed finances and businesses even in such families as the Fuggers.

Martin Luther loved and respected his wife for her gentle ministrations and ability. Soon after the first year of marriage, he wrote to a friend, "My Katie is in all things so obliging and pleasing to me that I would not exchange my poverty for the riches of Croesus." He even named Katherine the sole heir of his will instead of appointing a male guardian to administer his estate on behalf of her and her children, as was customary.

But even before Martin and Katherine began to establish their domestic household, trouble was brewing that would draw Luther back into the worldly fray. Thomas Müntzer was preaching a fiery brand of theology that, unlike Luther's, looked not to the apostles of the past but to revelation in the present. Müntzer rested his belief in the inward experience of the Spirit and a covenant of the elect, those who had been thus reborn. Much to Luther's outrage and horror, Müntzer averred that the elect would have to struggle with the ungodly.

In July 1523 Luther wrote his *Letter to the Princes of Saxony concerning the Rebellious Spirit,* in which he warned that Müntzer and his followers meant to foment an insurrection. Reiterating what had always been his position, Luther declared that the use of force can never be legitimized by invoking the Holy Spirit. One must endure differing religious views, Luther said, but when they lead to violence, the princes have a duty to act, to expel anyone promoting such violence. The battle should never be anything but spiritual.

Even before *To the Princes* appeared, however, Müntzer demonstrated that Luther's alarm was not unfounded. In a sermon delivered before Frederick the Wise and his brother Duke John, Müntzer had sought to enlist the princes in his cause. "The sword is given to you to wipe out the ungodly," Müntzer declared. "If you decline, it will be taken from you. Those who resist should be slaughtered without mercy." Within a few months Müntzer and other revolutionary leaders would rouse the peasantry to step forward and take up the sword.

At the beginning of their marriage, Luther wrote of Katherine von Bora *(above),* "I do not love my wife, but I appreciate her." Several years later, he told his now beloved spouse, "Katie, you have married an honest man who loves you; you are an empress."

Dürer's Door

As Martin Luther began the studies that would prepare him for his rift with Rome's theologians, Nürnberg artist Albrecht Dürer was forging a bond with Italy's painters. Twice he traveled to Venice to absorb the revival of classical art, which had not yet spread to his homeland. After immersing himself in Italian theories and techniques, Dürer—whose name is derived from a word that means door—almost single-handedly ushered the artistic Renaissance north.

A gifted and versatile artist who was blessed with a restless curiosity, Dürer explored with equal intensity and mastery the sacred and the profane—from a saint's apocalyptic vision to a mundane tuft of grass to an unprecedented series of self-portraits. Like Leonardo da Vinci, Albrecht Dürer transformed the role of artist from medieval craftsman to learned gentleman. Educator and theorist, painter and printmaker, humanist and businessman, but above all, individualist, Dürer typified the Renaissance man.

Dürer's stylish, flamboyant dress and elegant surroundings in this 1498 self-portrait proclaim the elevated status he felt an artist deserved. He wears the famed fine gray doeskin gloves of his birthplace of Nürnberg, but the alpine view in the background alludes to his sojourn in Italy.

"I have thus painted myself.

I was 26 years old."

Dürer's famous drawing, popularly known as The Praying Hands, was just one of many preparatory studies made for an altarpiece that had been commissioned by Frankfurt merchant Jacob Heller. The finished painting was destroyed in a fire, but the surviving sketch reveals Dürer's mastery of Renaissance techniques for rendering the human form.

The Artist as a Young Man

Albrecht Dürer was the third of 18 children born to a hardworking Nürnberg goldsmith and his wife. After a few years of grammar school, where he was taught reading, writing, arithmetic, and some Latin, young Albrecht entered his father's trade. In the family workshop, he learned to handle a goldsmith's tools, particularly the burin, an engraving tool used to produce designs on gold and silverware. Yet "my liking drew me more to painting," he later explained, so at the age of 15, he persuaded his father to apprentice him to artist Michael Wolgemut, who ran the city's largest commercial art workshop. There, in addition to the rudiments of painting, Dürer learned Wolgemut's pioneering techniques in woodcut design, and he honed his skills by copying prints by early Italian Renaissance masters.

Nürnberg was an ideal location for a young man with artistic talent, for it was at the center of European commerce and culture in the 15th and early 16th centuries. International trade brought a steady stream of foreign visitors and new ideas, not to mention the wealth that fostered artistic commissions and classical studies by resident humanists. The citizenry there was known for its ingenuity, and Nürnberg's industries—paper mills, printing presses, and copper-processing plants—produced the very resources necessary for an artist who was to become Germany's greatest printmaker.

After three years with Wolgemut, Dürer, like other young craftsmen, began his *Wanderjahre*, or "wander years," traveling and visiting other artists' workshops. Although he hoped to study with Martin Schongauer, the great German engraver had died the year before Dürer arrived. He continued his travels until 1494, when he was called home by his father to wed the daughter of a well-to-do Nürnberg craftsman. Yet within months, Dürer was off again, crossing the Alps to learn the techniques of the Italians firsthand.

A mill wheel leans against a copper-wire workshop in the foreground, and small villages dot the distance in this peaceful scene, one of Dürer's earliest watercolors. With its use of the customary browns, greens, and blues of Netherlandish landscapes, the work reflects the influence of traditional Dutch painting on Dürer's early work.

Working from his own image in a mirror, Dürer drew this remarkable likeness of himself when he was only 13 years old. The drawing, which young Albrecht completed using the difficult silverpoint technique—whereby an image is created by drawing on specially prepared paper with a silver stylus, permitting no erasures or corrections—is Dürer's earliest known work and may be the first self-portrait in European art.

From a vantage point at ground level, Dürer recorded every blade of grass, closed dandelion blossom, and oval leaf of plantain with clinical accuracy in this 1503 water-color, *Great Piece of Turf.* Like Leonardo da Vinci, Dürer had a lifelong fascination with portraying nature—he once wrote, "Art is rooted in Nature, and whoever can pull it out, has it."

A rendering of the mythic tale *The Abduction of Europa* fills the left half of this page of sketches by Dürer, while on the right, a Turkish alchemist examines a skull amid lion heads and an archer. In Italy, Dürer began to broaden his intellectual interests. He based his *Europa* on both the ancient story by Ovid and a sensuous retelling of the tale by Renaissance poet Angelo Poliziano.

The Effect of Classical Influences

Though German humanists had been traveling to Italy for many years to study the lessons of the rebirth of antiquity, such a trip was unheard of for a German artist. The northern European artistic tradition was strong, and painters chose to emulate the masters of Flanders rather than Tuscany. But remembering the Italian prints that he had painstakingly copied in Wolgemut's workshop, Dürer was drawn to the techniques and the vigor of Renaissance art and wished to apply them to his own work.

Dürer went to Venice, Europe's gateway to the Orient, a city that offered many lures in addition to art: sun and sea, luxurious goods and architecture, exotic travelers and "intelligent, . . . noble minds." Dürer immediately felt at peace there, "Here I am a gentleman," Dürer wrote, "at home only a parasite!" In Venice he began to refine his skill at rendering human proportion and perspective. He became intrigued with the concept of an ideal human form, and read Euclid and Vitruvius and experimented with geometry in an effort to determine ideal proportions.

The influence of Renaissance principles can be seen not only in the form of Dürer's art, but in the content and color as well. Upon his return to Germany, the nude entered his repertoire, along with antique drapery, mythological scenes, and classical pathos, and his once muted palette turned fresh and bright. Dürer's sojourn in Italy may truly be called the beginning of the Northern Renaissance.

The Bible's Four Horsemen—Death, Famine, Pestilence, and War—rampage forth in this scene from Dürer's *Apocalypse*, a collection of 15 woodcuts depicting the Revelation of Saint John. Published in 1498, the book of prints was a bestseller throughout Europe. Dürer expresses his vision of the Final Judgment in contemporary terms: outbreaks of the plague, invasion by the Turks, and a prophecy that the world would end in the year 1500. The specter of a bishop seized by the Dragon of Hell *(lower left)* warns that even church officials should fear Judgment Day.

"God gives much power to ingenious men."

The brooding figure in Dürer's *Melencolia I*—winged yet earthbound amid objects denoting the liberal arts—is considered to be a spiritual self-portrait of the artist, suggesting that melancholy is a major component of creative genius. One of the most enigmatic images in Renaissance art, it was engraved in 1514, the year Dürer's mother died.

Dürer the Printmaker

Back in Germany, Dürer opened his own shop. Instead of seeking commissions for portraits and altarpieces that required years of work and the accommodation of wealthy patrons, he took a different tack. Working in the medium of woodcuts and engravings, which could be produced quickly and which yielded hundreds of prints from each block or plate, Dürer amassed a stock of images on subjects of his own choosing. Since Nürnberg had no artists guild, the enterprising artist was free to engage an agent and sell his work anywhere he pleased.

Religious prints were much in demand. Aristocrats and middle-class burghers prayed to them, priests and nuns used them in lessons, artists and artisans copied them. So with the support of his godfather, printer Anton Koberger, Dürer published popular books of woodcuts on the Apocalypse, Christ's Passion, and the life of Mary. Although the themes were traditional, his techniques were revolutionary. Expanding on the innovations of Michael Wolgemut, Dürer's woodcuts realized their full potential—adding shape, volume, energy, and texture to what was once a flat and static medium.

Engravings, which yielded smaller editions than woodcuts, were Dürer's means of exploring secular and intellectual themes, such as myth and allegory, as well as personal visions, represented by his masterwork *Melencolia I*. Often intellectual and esoteric in nature, Dürer's engravings were prized by humanists throughout Europe.

For this self-portrait painted when he was 28, Dürer idealized his features and adopted a pose that casts him in the traditional image of Christ. His hair colored brown instead of its natural reddish blond and his right hand raised as if in blessing, Dürer purposely compares himself with Christ in celebration of his own role as a divinely endowed artist and creator.

Dürer and the Reformation

After Luther distributed his Ninety-five Theses, Nürnberg was in religious turmoil, and Dürer was not immune to the conflict. He deeply admired Luther, who had lifted him "out of great distress" after his mother's death. He even begged Erasmus to rescue Luther when he mistakenly thought the reformer's life was in danger. Yet even though the town council openly backed Luther's reforms, Dürer was reluctant to break with the church, which he hoped could be reformed.

In 1526 Dürer presented the council with the painting known as *The Four Apostles*. With this gift, he publicly expressed his affinity for Luther's ideas, for beneath the images of Saints John, Peter, Mark, and Paul are passages from Luther's translation of the New Testament, along with a warning to heed only the word of God.

When Dürer died two years later at the age of 57, Luther found comfort in thinking that the artist, who was "worthy to look on nothing but excellence," would be spared seeing "things most vile" in the troubling times to come.

Dürer's *Four Apostles* symbolizes the Lutheran belief in finding spiritual guidance from the Bible alone. A young Saint John *(left)* reads from his own gospel, "In the beginning was the Word . . . and the Word was God," to the older Saint Peter, who holds the key to the gates of heaven. At far right, Saint Mark stands behind the martyred Saint Paul, who holds a Bible and a sword.

CHAPTER TWO

Peasants and Princes Battle for Freedom

Spanish soldiers ruthlessly execute rebels in the Dutch town of Haarlem after securing the town's surrender by promising to pardon the insurgents. During the 16th century, war erupted across Germany and the Netherlands as princes and commoners battled for religious and political freedom.

uring the summer of 1524, German prince Philip of Hesse and his entourage set out from his castle at Marburg to attend a crossbow shoot in the town of Heidelberg. Passing through the forest known as the Odenwald, they happened upon another carriage. Philip soon discovered that its occupant was none other than Philipp Melanchthon, renowned theologian and colleague of Martin Luther. Excited, the landgrave, or ruler, of Hesse impulsively climbed into Melanchthon's carriage to pepper the theologian with questions.

The young prince had been reading Luther's controversial works and discussing them with his advisers, many of whom were enthusiastic Lutherans. After listening to the scholarly and persuasive Melanchthon, Philip drove on to Heidelberg a proud new convert to Lutheranism. Only 20 years of age, he was still possessed of the exuberance and rashness of youth, with little thought for the danger involved in his rejection of the Catholic Church.

Philip had already been tested by adversity. In 1508, at age four, he had lost his father, the previous landgrave, and had immediately become the center of a power struggle. Hesse, a mountain-and-forest-studded area of about 13,500 square miles in west-central Germany, was a prize worth controlling, and rebellious nobles managed to seize the regency from the boy's mother, Anna, and separate mother and son. But Anna fought back. By the end of 1513, she had garnered enough support in the towns and among the imperial knights to re-claim her son and the regency. Seeing her enemies once more clamoring to take control of Philip a few years later, Anna thwarted their ambitions by asking Emperor Maximilian I to declare Philip's early majority, allowing him to become landgrave at age 14. Five years afterward, the ruler helped defeat a group of rebels in the Knights' War, when a small force of impoverished knights attempted to seize land in central, western, and southern Germany.

The determined and aggressive landgrave would find himself embroiled in many more conflicts in the years following his religious conversion. Inspired by Luther and the Reformation, peasants and princes alike would rise up to challenge the established order for political and religious freedom.

In Germany, Philip would rouse his fellow Protestant rulers to battle for their beliefs against the might of the Holy Roman Emperor Charles V. In the Netherlands, Spanish king Philip II's desire for political domination and his fanatical persecution of non-Catholics would incite a revolt and bring forth an unlikely hero, William of Orange. Born in Germany, raised by Charles V to be a devoted Catholic and subject, the wealthy and pleasure-loving William would risk everything to lead the Netherlanders in their bid for independence.

Yet long before the battle of the emperor and the German princes and the struggle

In the German countryside, noblemen hunt deer, a pastime that proved a double burden on peasants, who often were made to assist the hunters while the noblemen's horses trampled their crops. To ensure that wild game had the run of the land, lords forced peasants to leave their fields unfenced and to hobble their dogs.

between the Netherlanders and the Spanish king, another cry for justice rang out. It came not from the nobility, but from the German peasants, who revolted against their ecclesiastical and secular lords. And the man who would ride against them was Philip of Hesse.

In June 1524 local peasants in southwestern Germany received a summons from the countess of Stühlingen demanding that they abandon their own harvests to pick strawberries and collect the snail shells on which the ladies of the manor wound their thread. Outraged, the peasants stopped work, formed a band 1,000 strong under a former mercenary soldier, and began enlisting aid from nearby towns in their attempts to negotiate with the count of Stühlingen, Sigmund von Lupfen, for justice.

The imperious order for berries and shells was only the final straw tossed on a load of services and financial exactions the peasants in Stühlingen—like those in other parts of Germany—found increasingly unbearable. The demands were exacerbated by a growing denial of traditional privileges and rights as German lords, for whom the peasants were contracted workers, sought greater revenues and political power. Among many other actions, they were denying people the right to sell commercial crops in certain markets and forcing them to sell products to their lords at lesser prices.

The count, like others, was also denying the peasants access to fields and forests that previously had been common lands. For most peasants, who were subsistence farmers, usage of such lands was crucial for grazing animals, gathering firewood, cutting timber for building, and hunting and fishing. Now rulers were leasing or selling those lands for private use. They were also leasing the streams running through the peasants' fields to well-to-do fishermen, who, the Stühlingen peasants complained, "have inflicted grave damage on our properties by tearing down dams and weirs, thus making it impossible for us to use our mills and water our meadows."

Unlike Count Sigmund, Philip of Hesse was a relatively enlightened ruler, yet his subjects had their own grievances. The landgrave owned most of the sheep that produced Hesse's main export, raw wool, and dominated the pastures at the expense of the peasants. Use of the forests was also a sticking point. One of his treasury agents required that peasants bring him the best timber as part of their compulsory labor obligation to the landgrave. Instead of utilizing the wood for fortifications or other state purposes, as they had been led to believe, the agent had it made into furniture to be sold in Frankfurt.

Seeking stricter, more-centralized political authority, lords were replacing traditional village courts and laws with their own courts and Roman law. Taxes were levied to pay the unwanted new court officials, or officials were granted the area's feudal dues as payment, giving them an incentive to raise exactions. Grievances were exacerbated when rulers were clerics who did not hesitate to use canon law and the threat of excommunication to control people.

When Count Sigmund refused the peasants' demands, what had begun as a kind of strike became a revolt, spreading eastward from Stühlingen along the northern shore of Lake Constance into the south-central duchy of Swabia and northward through the Odenwald. During the winter, the uprising spilled over into parts of Switzerland and Austria. In late February 1525, in the Swabian town of Memmingen, a peasant alliance, citing the gospel as its guide, drafted an extraordinary document that came to be known as the Twelve Articles. It called for the right of local parishes to elect their own

copies of the Twelve Articles were printed and circulated as a rallying cry for peasants. The rebels, looking to Luther for support, sent him a copy. While agreeing that some complaints were just, Luther, who saw the cause as a legal, not a religious, problem, advised the peasants to appeal for help to German lords sympathetic to justice and peace. At the same time, Luther warned the rulers of Germany to take heed of the rebels' legitimate complaints or be prepared to pay an awful price. "The peasants are mustering, and this must result in the ruin, destruction, and desolation of Germany by cruel murder and bloodshed."

Neither side listened. Many nobles blamed Luther's Reformation for the storm, while the peasants branded him a traitor for telling them to resign themselves to the shackles of serfdom because Jesus Christ granted the freedom of only their spirits, not their bodies. By

"*Remember the command of God to Moses to destroy utterly and show no mercy!*"

pastors, an end to serfdom, reduction of dues and labor obligations, free collection of wood, abolition of certain tithes, and restoration of hunting and fishing rights.

Two of these articles were truly revolutionary. The first, the continuing right to choose and dismiss local pastors, was heretofore unheard of. Even Luther believed only in a community's right to establish evangelical preachers in the place of Catholic priests, not ongoing choice. And second, the demand for an end to serfdom went against what was, in the eyes of the law, an unbreakable contract. But the Swabian peasants argued, "It has been the custom hitherto for men to hold us as their own property, and this is pitiable, seeing that Christ has redeemed and bought us all with the precious shedding of His blood, the lowly as well as the great."

During the following weeks, 25 separate editions and 25,000

the spring of 1525, an estimated 300,000 peasants had taken up the cause. In armies as large as 15,000 men, they demolished castles and burned monasteries and convents after plundering the well-stocked cellars and storehouses.

On April 16, 1525, Easter Sunday, peasants in the market town of Weinsberg, southeast of Heidelberg, staged a spectacle in which, wrote a parson, "Lucifer and all his angels were let loose." They forced the count to run a lethal gauntlet, striking out at him with lances and accusations.

"You caused the hands of my father to be cut off because he killed a hare on his own field!" cried one man. Another yelled out, "You thrust my brother into a dungeon because he did not bare his head as you passed by!" Once the count fell to his wounds, other nobles were forced to run the gauntlet as well.

To Philip of Hesse, the rebels had "dealt so unchristianly and evilly with Count Ludwig von Helfenstein . . . that it is piteous and hard to relate." A few days later, the revolt reached his own backyard, erupting in towns just beyond Hesse's eastern border. These rebels then sought alliances with Hessian peasants.

"If we do not counter such wanton people with seriousness and boldness," Philip wrote his father-in-law, Duke George of Albertine Saxony, "then it is a sure and fearful certainty that . . . all authority must expect the next slap in the face." Moving decisively, the prince quelled the revolt within his own borders before marching northward to meet the duke's forces and strike at a hotbed of revolt: Mühlhausen. Some 80 miles northeast of Marburg, Mühlhausen was technically an imperial free city but in practice had become a protectorate of the princes of Hesse on the west and Saxony on the east.

In Mühlhausen, the rebellion blazed at full pitch. The leader of this uprising was

Peasants attack and plunder the monastery of Weisenau in Hesse, some killing monks, some making off with provisions, others swilling the monks' liquor, and a few netting fish in the monastery's pond. In the Peasants' War of the mid-1520s, people angered by unfair restrictions and demands for additional service assaulted their lords, whose ranks comprised monks as well as nobles.

Thomas Müntzer, the fiery 35-year-old former Franciscan priest who had broken with Luther and was now his foremost German critic and would-be rival for leadership of the Reformation. Müntzer, unlike Luther, saw no distinction between theology and politics. "The princes bleed the people with usury and count as their own the fish in the stream, the bird of the air, and the grass of the field," Müntzer said. Every person should receive according to his or her need, he continued. "Any prince, count, or lord who refuses to do this even when seriously warned should be hanged or have his head chopped off."

Müntzer won election as pastor at Mühlhausen's Church of St. Mary. His rhetoric resonated powerfully with peasants, miners, and artisans. They deposed the city council and elected a new one, expelled the clergy, and closed all monastic institutions. An army that Müntzer christened the Eternal League of God began assembling from the town as well as from the surrounding countryside. From the pulpit of St. Mary's, Müntzer unfurled a long white silk banner emblazoned with a rainbow—the biblical symbol for the covenant God had made with humanity after the Flood. He exhorted his listeners: "Remember the command of God to Moses to destroy utterly and show no mercy!"

On April 26 Müntzer and a few hundred followers marched out of Mühlhausen under their rainbow banner. Like other rebel armies, this one had many experienced soldiers but no veteran officers. They were poorly equipped, brandishing pikes, swords, and even farming tools; fewer than one in 10 carried firearms. There was no cavalry or artillery. But over the next couple of weeks, they faced little opposition from nobles and ecclesiastics as they sacked a score or more of castles and convents, initially in the local area and then in a series of forays to the northwest. By mid-May, they had joined a large force encamped at Frankenhausen, about 30 miles north of Mühlhausen. Quickly accepted as the leader of some 8,000 rebels, Müntzer preached that God was on their side.

On May 15 the rebels drew up on a hill east of town and surrounded themselves with a barricade of wagons. Philip's cavalry and foot soldiers approached from the west while Duke George's Saxons moved in from the east. Müntzer rode around the encampment rallying his people. The princes sent in a demand that the rebels give up Müntzer, promising to spare everyone else. While the peasants debated, Müntzer pointed to the sky. A halo was taking shape around the sun, resembling

MÜNSTER'S ANABAPTISTS

The caged corpses of religious radical John of Leiden and two of his followers hang from a church spire in the city of Münster after their execution in 1536. John had briefly ruled as Münster's "king" after the city was taken over by Anabaptists, Christian sectarians who practiced adult baptism and often sought to separate themselves from society.

Although their number was small, the German Anabaptists' refusal to swear civil oaths and provide military service worried authorities, who saw treason in such defiance and feared it could lead to anarchy. These fears were exacerbated by the extremist behavior of the Münster Anabaptists, who practiced polygamy and advocated communal ownership of goods. Catholic and Protestant rulers, including Philip of Hesse, joined forces to besiege the city; 15 months later, the kingdom of Münster was no more.

the rainbow on their banner. This, he shouted, was a divine sign of impending victory.

The Hessians and Saxons opened fire. The first cannon shots fell short, and Müntzer cried, "I told you, no shots will harm you." But as the enemy attacked in force, the peasants panicked and scattered. Most of them immediately fell to the attackers, but some managed to slip inside the town. A Hessian count later reported, "We began to storm the town at once and conquered it speedily, and killed everyone caught there." The princely forces reportedly lost six men, the rebels nearly 6,000. Müntzer took refuge in an attic, where he allegedly was found in bed, pretending to be "a poor sick man."

The princes then marched on Mühlhausen. Near the city they were met first by hundreds of women, then by men, all of whom knelt to beg for mercy. The older women wore humble clothes, while the maidens were bedecked with wormwood garlands—a traditional way of expressing penitence. The men were barefoot and bareheaded. Müntzer was brought back to the surrendered city, where Philip demanded the rebel leader acknowledge his guilt. Müntzer was so weak from torture he could hardly speak, but he refused, urging instead that the princes stop burdening the peasants. On May 27 he was beheaded, his head and body then impaled upon a pike and put on display as a public lesson.

By the time the Peasants' War sputtered out during the summer of 1526, an estimated 100,000 rebels had lost their lives. Survivors suffered reprisals ranging from heavy fines and penalty taxes to the draconian decree of Prince Casimir of Brandenburg for the deliberate blinding of 62 citizens of the town of Kitzingen, on the pretext they had refused "to look upon him" as their lord. In many places the maiming and impoverishment of the peasants stopped only after their lords realized they risked cutting off the hand that fed them. A few princes, Philip in particular, wisely made concessions. Philip limited the ability of nobles to increase dues and rents. He established territorial hospitals to serve the peasantry, launched a public-school system, and founded a university at Marburg with scholarships for the lower classes.

With the end of the Peasants' War, Philip could turn to strengthening his new religion. He had monastic orders in Hesse dissolved and began building a territory-wide church that preached his new evangelical faith. He also became a leading advocate of Lutheranism among his fellow princes. Duke George of Saxony and other Catholic nobles, blaming the war on the new faith as Luther had feared, had formed an alliance aimed at preventing future uprisings and at suppressing the "damned Lutheran sect." Philip retaliated by forming an evangelical alliance of towns and principalities for mutual assistance if any one of them was attacked for religious reasons. When nobles, prelates, and delegates gathered in the city of Speyer in 1526 for the empire's annual meeting of the diet, the headstrong young prince flaunted his new faith and outraged Catholics by staging an ox barbecue on Friday, the day on which meat traditionally was taboo. In 1529, when the diet was again held in Speyer, he opposed the pro-Catholic decrees and orchestrated the evangelical protests that gave the new faith a new name—Protestantism.

On June 15, 1530, Philip found himself in Augsburg, participating in a great spectacle. Astride his horse, he stood among 120 Hessian crossbowmen clad in gray. Their arms bore the motto V.D.M.I.E., which they explained stood for *Verbum dei manet in eternum*—"God's Word endures forever"—though Catholics joked that it really meant *vnd du musst ins elend*—"and you must get out of town." Along with over 1,000 representatives of the city and other principalities, they were lined up near the bridge over the Lech River to welcome back Emperor Charles V. The 30-year-old emperor had been away from Germany for nearly a decade, preoccupied with wars against the French and the Turks.

Charles was returning to preside at the Diet of Augsburg,

hoping to settle the religious schism that divided Germany. The pomp and power of his position were on full display. With him came a horde of courtiers and clergy from all over his far-flung empire. There were 1,000 infantry, 500 riders in full armor, a bodyguard of 300, and even 200 Spanish hunting dogs. At the bridge, Charles dismounted and graciously greeted each of the princes, including Philip. The emperor then continued on to the cathedral in glorious procession under a red, white, and green canopy carried by six magistrates of the city.

As he rode toward the cathedral in pageantry symbolizing the might of the Holy Roman Empire, Philip must have felt skeptical about the proceedings. He doubted that Charles could be objective—after all, he had sworn to uphold the Roman Catholic faith—and in any event Philip denied that the emperor had jurisdiction in religious matters. When the procession reached the cathedral, both Philip and his ally, Elector John of Ernestine Saxony, refused to kneel or remove their hats during the service.

That evening, the emperor summoned the Protestant princes. When his brother, Ferdinand, demanded that their pastors cease preaching in Augsburg, they balked. They also refused to participate in the following day's religious procession. Philip's colleague Margrave George of Brandenburg stepped forward and declared:

"Before I would deny my God and His Gospel I would rather kneel down here before Your Imperial Majesty and let you cut off my head."

Charles suffered such impertinence because he wanted the help of these rebellious nobles against the Turks of the Ottoman Empire. He agreed to allow the Protestants to prepare a written defense. This document was drafted by Philip's old religious mentor Philipp Melanchthon. Martin Luther, who was still under imperial ban and could be arrested if he showed himself, sent suggestions and encouragement almost daily. When Melanchthon despaired of striking just the right note of conciliation, Luther tried to reassure him by saying the worst that could befall the Protestant negotiators was execution.

The finished work, known to history as the Augsburg Confession, became an important exposition of Lutheran theology and its definitive creed. It required two hours to be read aloud to the emperor, and by at least two accounts, he dozed off. The Catholics prepared a rebuttal, and to no one's surprise, Charles came down on their side. By the time he issued an edict ordering the dissidents—John of electoral Saxony, Philip of Hesse, four other princes, and six free cities—to return to the fold of the mother church by April 1531, Philip had already left in disgust. The Reformation

had gone too far to be willed away by the emperor.

Philip and his allies formed a new alliance to defend Protestantism—with the sword, if necessary. Founded in the Thuringian town of Schmalkald and known as the Schmalkaldic League, this federation soon embraced a half-dozen principalities and more than a dozen cities. Charles was too busy fighting the Turks to enforce his Augsburg ultimatum or confront the league. In 1534, Philip further undercut the emperor's influence in southern Germany by helping the Protestant duke Ulrich recover his duchy at Württemberg, which had been in Hapsburg hands for 15 years. The future of the alliance looked promising—until Philip, its foremost proponent, gave its enemies a potent weapon to wield against it: bigamy.

A cavalcade of princes, pages, nobles, and knights *(below)* escorts Holy Roman Emperor Charles V into Augsburg for the opening of the 1530 diet. Above, the chapter hall of the bishop's palace in Augsburg is filled to capacity as the Saxon chancellor reads the Augsburg Confession, which summarized Lutheran theology, to Charles and the members of the diet.

Wed before he was 19 in a political match to Duke George's daughter Christina, Philip had a desperately unhappy marriage. "From the time when I first took her," he said later, "I neither desired nor wished her because of her unattractive appearance, disposition, and reputation, and besides she was subject to spells of excessive intemperance." This did not prevent him from fathering many children with her, but it did cause him to find solace with a series of prostitutes. His conscience so troubled him because of his untamed

libido that he declined to take part in Communion, fearing that to do so would damn his soul.

Another consequence of his promiscuity was venereal disease. By 1539 Philip was beset by attacks of syphilis and conscience so severe that he decided to take drastic action. Divorce was out of the question. Luther would not allow it, and the heretic prince could hardly seek permission for an annulment from the pope. His sister Elisabeth suggested that, to solve the problem of promiscuity, he "take one bedmate instead of the many whores." Philip heeded that advice, but not exactly in the manner his sister had meant. Instead of a mistress, he took another wife.

He had become enamored of his sister's 17-year-old lady-in-waiting, Margaret of Saale, and in 1539 decided to marry her—a decision no doubt influenced by Margaret's mother, who agreed to the union only if Philip promised an honorable Christian marriage. Taking an attractive wife, he reasoned, meant he would not again be tempted to adultery. Philip wanted approval at the highest level and through an adviser approached Luther and Melanchthon.

Luther, who believed in divorce only when the mate had committed adultery or desertion, pondered the issue. He wanted to help Philip and remembered the Old Testament patriarchs who had practiced bigamy and even polygamy without divine displeasure. So in December 1539, he advised Philip, and Melanchthon concurred, that the second marriage would be permissible if kept secret—a wise precaution since just eight years before, Charles V had made bigamy a crime punishable by death.

With Luther's blessing, Philip forged ahead. He got his first wife to agree to the bigamous solution on the promise that her children would be his heirs and he would continue to render her "friendliness." (He kept his promise, giving her three additional children—bringing the total to 10—before her death a decade later.) In March 1540 he

These woodcut portraits of Philip of Hesse, right, and his first wife, Christina of Saxony, above, date from about 1535, when Philip was at the peak of his power. Philip defeated his own efforts to build Hesse into a major state by arranging for it to be divided among his four legitimate sons after his death.

married Margaret before witnesses that included Melanchthon. Despite the need for secrecy, the bride's mother was soon bragging to others about the wedding. Elisabeth, Philip's sister, was so angered by his actions that she, too, refused to keep quiet. Now that the secret was becoming public, Luther and the other theologians backed away from their earlier approval. Luther urged a "strong denial" and concealment of the marriage contract. But Philip defended it publicly.

Abandoned by his supposed allies, Philip decided to make peace with the emperor to avoid a possible death sentence. In 1541 Philip and Charles concluded a treaty. The emperor promised not to prosecute Philip and not to undertake any war against Hesse on account of religion—unless he attacked all the Protestant states. Philip, in return, would halt all attempts to strengthen the Schmalkaldic League and to desist from activities against the emperor.

Though this agreement neutralized the league's foremost champion, Charles was too distracted by foreign wars to take advantage of it. For a time, German Protestants could go their own way without fear.

While Philip of Hesse struggled to adjust to his new political impotence, a young Protestant from northern Germany was just getting started in the turbulent world of the Reformation. In June 1542 Bartholomew Sastrow, the 22-year-old second son of a prosperous brewer and merchant, left his home in Stralsund, in the duchy of Pomerania on the Baltic Sea. With his older brother, John, young Bartholomew headed for Speyer, some 400 miles away, intending to seek his fortune and keep an eye on a family lawsuit in the imperial court there.

Bartholomew was in high spirits, which soared when he and John reached Wittenberg. The brothers were sturdy Lutherans—Pomerania was an early northern stronghold of the new faith—and John had studied theology at the town's university. As they rode past a bookshop near the cemetery, John spotted Martin Luther. Excited, the brothers stopped to shake hands, and soon after, Luther's associates gave them letters of introduction to Speyer's lawyers.

The letters enabled Bartholomew Sastrow to get a favorable position as a scribe, copying documents for an eminent procurator of the imperial court—"a most learned lawyer and excellent practitioner," the young man noted with pride. Bartholomew was well prepared, having studied for two years at the university in Rostock, a seaport 41 miles southwest of his hometown. But this auspicious beginning faded after four months. The procurator had to reduce his staff because the Protestant states had renounced the imperial court, and Bartholomew lost his job.

He soon found service with Simeon Engelhardt, his father's legal advocate at the court. The litigation, brought by the elder Sastrow over a business matter involving the sale of draper's cloth, had made its way through the local court and council back home in Stralsund, then on to the appellate court at Lübeck, and finally to Speyer. Although Bartholomew Sastrow's new position allowed him to monitor the lawsuit (which would not be resolved for three decades), the duties turned out to be more than he bargained for. He later complained, "I might as well have taken service in Hell."

In addition to handling documents in some 400 lawsuits, each document of which had to be copied four times by him or the other clerk, Sastrow was treated by his employer's wife as a household servant. She had him teach her eight-year-old son German grammar, set and clear the table, throw out the dishwater, shop for cabbages, turnips, bread, and other daily staples, pump the water on laundry day, and climb down the well to repair the pump when it malfunctioned. She skimped on his food—"a piece of meat not as big as an egg" and a single goblet of wine—and forbade his leaving the household without permission. "Her dreadful character," he wrote, "inspired me from that day forward with an aversion for petticoat government."

Sastrow's job did give him a front-row seat for observing the emperor. He wrote that when Charles arrived during the autumn

Calvin and the Fire of Rebellion

Frail, somewhat shy, and sensitive, French theologian John Calvin, born in 1509, seemed an unlikely revolutionary. But he had a powerful intellect and deep convictions, and after converting to Protestantism at age 24, he added to the fire of evangelical rebellion blazing across Europe.

In 1536, after fleeing Catholic France for more tolerant Switzerland, Calvin outlined his beliefs in the *Institutes of the Christian Religion.* He held that church doctrine should be based solely on Scripture and that the church should enforce proper behavior among people. He also believed in predestination: A person's salvation or damnation was a decision God had predetermined, all people could do was believe and trust in God and live as the Bible commanded. With his writings, Calvin brought a new level of organization and structure to the Reform movement. He then restructured the workings of an entire city according to Calvinist principles.

Geneva, having ejected its Catholic overlord, asked Calvin to help carry out its reformation. With the city council, he and church officials instituted a strict regime, regulating every aspect of the Genevans' lives. They passed laws restricting activities such as gambling, drinking, dancing, and card playing. At the same time, Calvin improved charitable services and hospitals. Protestants flocked to Geneva, where Calvin trained them in his academy. By 1564, when the theologian died, his students were spreading his teachings throughout France, Scotland, and the Netherlands and fomenting revolt.

John Calvin *(left)* once confessed to another theologian that his own greatest moral struggle was "the wild beast of his wrath," which could rear its head when someone opposed him.

On simple benches in a sparsely furnished church in Lyon, France, a Calvinist congregation listens to a preacher, whose sermon is timed by an hourglass dangling to his right.

of 1543, he had a run-in with a teamster. The man and his wagon were moving too slowly down the road for the emperor, who rapped the wagoner with the imperial riding crop. The teamster, not knowing the identity of his assailant, struck back with his whip. Charles was content to have the man's nose cut off instead of hanging him. The teamster "bore the operation with a good grace," wrote Sastrow, "and for the remainder of his life sang the praises of the emperor."

Supply wagons and a large contingent of servants, tradespeople, and other camp followers straggle after a 16th-century imperial army on the move. The women in such a group often served as cooks, nurses, laundresses, and sexual partners.

During Lent early in 1544, Sastrow watched while the emperor performed the ritual of washing the feet of 12 poor men. Sastrow noted that "their feet had been washed beforehand" and the sovereign "merely dried the feet." Bartholomew's brother John composed a poem in honor of the emperor, who during that March conferred upon the older Sastrow brother the title of poet laureate.

Two months later, Bartholomew himself received his diploma as an imperial notary and took off for greener pastures, which he found the following year north of Speyer, near the city of Mainz, in the imperial town of Niederweisel. Sastrow found employment as a notary with the receiver—collector of revenues—for a Catholic organization of knights, the Order of St. John. The handsomely paid receiver had retired from the Turkish wars and was enjoying a frolicsome old age with a retinue that included his 18-year-old mistress, a debauched chaplain, a fool, three huntsmen, fine Frisian stallions, and an ancient monkey. "Gaming, feasting and drinking took up all the time," Sastrow noted. After three years of poverty, he did not stint on himself. "Well fitting clothes, a sword with a silver sheath-tip, and a golden ring on my little finger contributed greatly to transform me into a young gallant."

Early in 1546, Bartholomew Sastrow received news that his brother, John, had died in Rome, where he had gone after an unhappy love affair. To recover his brother's property, Sastrow set out for the papal city in April. His employer advised the young traveler "to abstain in Italy, but above all in Rome, from all theological controversy." It was good advice. In Italy, just being a German was grounds for suspicion of heresy. When he was stopped by magistrates and questioned about his religion, Sastrow lied, saying that he was a Catholic.

In Rome, Sastrow discovered the Inquisition was raging at fever pitch, routing out heretics and stirring up the

ardor of Catholics. It was in the papal city, in a boardinghouse run by an old Swedish priest, that Sastrow heard of the death of Martin Luther. At mealtime one day, the priest announced with satisfaction that the Reformer "had met with the end he deserved; a legion of devils had swooped down upon him, and a horrible din had put all those around him to flight."

When Sastrow left the city in July 1546, the long-awaited war between the emperor and the Schmalkaldic League was about to erupt. Charles V, having concluded a treaty with the French and a truce with the Turks, was preparing to crack down at last on Philip of Hesse and his allied rebels. Knowing the roads would be swarming with Italian mercenaries recruited by Pope Paul III to aid the emperor, Sastrow took great pains to look like one of them—"I had my sword by my side and a rosary dangling from the belt, like a soldier joining his regiment." He had also arranged to travel with a German companion named Nicholas, who spoke excellent Italian and would do all the talking for them, while Sastrow pretended to be mute.

German mercenaries, known as *Landsknechte*, were notorious enough. But Sastrow found the Italian mercenaries to be even "greater ruffians." He and his companion were eating in an inn near the Italian city of Viterbo when a band of mercenaries threw the owner out the door and then pillaged his larder and drank his wine. Before leaving they staved in the wine barrels in the cellar.

Evidently taking a liking to the disguised Germans, the mercenaries insisted upon accompanying them to Viterbo. Sastrow and his friend parted from their unwanted companions as soon as possible. But the town was awash in papal recruits, forcing a fearful Sastrow and his friend to shun the lodgings where such mercenaries usually stayed and go door to door seeking lodging from the townspeople—with no luck. As they wandered down yet another street that night, "a man of forty and of excellent appearance" approached them. Despite their dress he immediately identified them as German and warned that if the town's chief magistrate got hold of them he would put them on the rack. "Let me put you into the right road," the stranger insisted and escorted them to the city gates, prevailing upon the guard there to open up before dawn so they could escape. The astonished duo never learned the identity of their mysterious benefactor.

Soon their Italian disguises became a liability. Near the Austrian border, they ran into a group of miners who, "though by no means devout, after all preferred Luther to the pope." Spotting the pair's clothing and soldierlike equipment, they shook their spears and shouted, "Kill the papists!" After revealing their identities, Sastrow and his companion changed into German dress. In southern Germany, they passed through the lines of the emperor's forces awaiting a full-scale attack from the Protestants in the north. But it was an attack that never came, because one of the Protestant princes, Duke Maurice of Albertine Saxony, the son-in-law of Philip of Hesse, decided to side with the emperor, forcing his former allies to turn back and defend their own dominions.

Safely back in Stralsund, Sastrow took a job in the ducal chancellery that soon thrust him into a vital diplomatic mission related to the Schmalkaldic War. In the spring of 1547, he accompanied the chancellor on a mission to persuade the emperor that, while the two dukes of Pomerania had indeed joined the Schmalkaldic League a decade previously, they had remained neutral during the war. This mission was crucial because the emperor had crushed the Protestants, sealing his victory on the battlefield at Mühlberg, near Wittenberg, in April.

A few days later, Sastrow rode through this area where the Protestant

A crimson sash and saddlecloth proclaim Charles V a champion of Catholicism *(below, left)* in a Titian portrait painted to commemorate the emperor's victory over Philip of Hesse and the Protestant Schmalkaldic League at the Battle of Mühlberg *(left).*

elector of Saxony, John Frederick (son of Philip of Hesse's original ally, Elector John), had suffered defeat and surrendered. "Wherever the eye turned there were signs of the recent battle; broken lances, shattered muskets, and torn-up harnesses littered the ground, and all along the road soldiers dying of their wounds and from want of sustenance." Sastrow had hidden the yellow armor neckpiece, or gorget, that symbolized the Protestant cause and replaced it with the red gorget of the imperial forces. A Spanish soldier—one among many who made up about one-third of the imperial army there—noted the new gorget and observed, "Your service with the emperor is but of recent date." Sastrow rode a little further, then stopped to rub the gorget against his boot to make it appear less new.

Nearly three months later, Sastrow was in the Saxon city of Halle when Philip of Hesse surrendered. He had been assured by his turncoat son-in-law Maurice that the emperor would treat

him lightly. But in fact Charles wanted the rebel prince's humiliation. In June 1547 Philip knelt while his chancellor read out an apology. The emperor noted that Philip smiled with an air of bravado during the reading. Charles pointed his finger and exclaimed, "Go on; I'll teach you to laugh!" It was not an empty threat. For the next five years, Philip would be confined to the imperial city of Donauwörth, in Bavaria, where he would be accompanied by Spanish guards at all times. "I recommend to my children submission to the authorities," Sastrow wrote many years later. "For the good of their soul and the welfare of their body they ought never to make pacts with sedition-mongers."

Sastrow was an eyewitness to history two years later when the emperor's 22-year-old son, Philip, came to Speyer in June 1549. In reward for his successful mission for his dukes, Sastrow had been named Pomerania's solicitor at the imperial court in Speyer. Looking at young Philip, Sastrow felt that "his far from intellectual face gave little hope of his equalling his father one day." Unlike his broad-shouldered father, Philip was short and thin. And in contrast to the emperor, who was gracious to his nobles, Sastrow thought the son "was most exacting with the electors and the princes, though many of them were old men." In 1550 Sastrow returned to Pomerania to go into private practice and marry, and there he would live until his death 53 years later.

In 1552, two years after Sastrow's return home, the Protestant princes staged another revolt. This time Duke Maurice, who had become appalled at the emperor's treatment of his imprisoned father-in-law, led the way. The Protestants freed Philip of Hesse and John Frederick of Saxony and drove Charles from Germany, winning freedom of worship for Lutherans and the right to govern their own territories within the framework of a weakened empire.

Having failed in Germany, Charles decided to begin abdicating his various offices in 1555. Ferdinand, his brother, would receive Germany and Austria and the title emperor. His son would become Philip II, king of Spain, a title that included sovereign authority over the Netherlands, Charles's birthplace.

In October, a prematurely aged Charles returned to Brussels for the transfer of power over the Netherlands, also known as the Low Countries. Clad simply in black, his white hair clipped close, his once athletic body crippled by gout, the 55-year-old emperor limped into the ceremony in the great hall of the palace with one gnarled hand on his walking stick and the other on the shoulder of his favorite young prince, the sturdy and handsome 22-year-old William of Orange. The ruler-to-be—the unimposing Philip—walked behind. Charles hoped that William, a popular nobleman in the Netherlands, would support and advise Philip in his new reign.

Born and raised in Spain, Philip II spoke neither Dutch nor French, believed in the absolute power of kings, and was a fervent

Tired hunters and their dogs return from a winter expedition *(below)*. In the background, townspeople roast a pig in preparation for a village feast.

Balancing baskets of freshly picked cherries and vegetables on their heads, a group of peasants travels the road to market, while in the distance, workers in a hayfield rake freshly mown grass *(far left)*. At near left, three girls carrying rakes head home after a long day's work.

Peasants in the Low Countries

Peasant life in the 16th-century Netherlands, or Low Countries, varied widely from one location to another. In northeastern Gelderland and southern provinces such as Luxembourg, for instance, serfdom was still in place, and peasants there served and paid taxes to the landowning church and nobility. In other regions, such as Flanders and Brabant, peasants led a somewhat freer existence. Their ancestors had been released from serfdom as early

as the 12th century, when the Catholic Church and wealthy aristocrats began offering freedom and lease agreements to local farmers to stem migration to Germany and give people an incentive to work land newly reclaimed from the sea. In the northern-most provinces of Friesland and Groningen, the feudal system did not take hold because the rich never owned much land there.

Sixteenth-century peasants worked at

a variety of occupations. Many farmed, growing grain and other crops for themselves as well as for market in nearby towns or raising industrial crops such as flax or hemp to support the burgeoning textile industry. Stock farming was a lucrative pursuit, and wealthier farmers—not all peasants were poor—amassed as many cattle as they could afford. Other individuals sought opportunities as artisans or day workers in cities and towns.

Most peasants lived in thatch-roofed cottages with one large ground-level room and a hearth. God-fearing and wary of strangers, they looked to their neighbors for companionship and eagerly awaited the yearly round of such seasonal feast days and holidays as Twelfth Night, Whitsuntide, or May Day. In November families gathered to slaughter an ox or a pig purchased at a cattle fair to sustain them throughout the cold winter months.

The kermis was the most popular annual celebration—later held twice a year—an ancient Dutch traditional festival celebrated in the village square on the feast day of the local patron saint. For as long as a week, people gathered from near and far, buying trinkets and wares from traveling merchants, sharing meals, laughing, talking, and dancing in the streets with abandon. Excessive drinking usually took its toll, though, as brawls over a card game or a misinterpreted glance commonly spilled onto the streets. The fights caused havoc, and raised disapproving remarks from a contingent of stern onlookers, many of whom attended the kermis just to observe the debauchery.

A basketful of earthenware jugs at the ready, a man cheerfully pours out beer for a wedding feast. Sitting nearby, a little girl enjoys the food, clutching her bowl in one hand and holding a roll safely in her lap.

During a boisterous Flemish kermis, a bagpiper plays a lively tune for dancing couples while other celebrants drink and a man and woman share an earthy kiss.

Catholic, with no tolerance for other religions. Those characteristics made him ill prepared for ruling the Netherlands, where each of the 17 provinces (comprising modern-day Holland, Belgium, Luxembourg, and part of France) had its own laws, courts, nobility, traditions, and even languages—from French in southern cities like Tournai to Low German and various dialects of Dutch. Within the provinces there were counties, duchies, seigneuries, and independent cities, many with their own constitutional charters, courts, guilds, and governing bodies.

Like his father, Philip became the sovereign for each province, since there was no king of the Netherlands as a whole. But the only real authority the royal government had was control over the army and the power to appoint the stadholder, or leading officer, of each province and the chief magistrates of the cities. If the king wished

"We want the prince of Orange!"

to institute new policies or request funds, he had to present his proposals to provincial representatives for acceptance or rejection.

It was a political system Philip hated, much as he hated the Protestantism found among his new subjects. Though the majority of Netherlanders were Catholic, theirs was a more tolerant faith than that practiced by Philip and his fellow Spaniards. Philip's father had done his best to stamp out Lutheranism in the Netherlands. Philip was faced with a more powerful second generation of religious reformers—the Calvinists, who were pouring into the Netherlands from the south.

Philip soon enacted harsher edicts against heresy and established several new bishoprics. To these new dioceses he appointed bishops with great religious zeal, who would rigorously persecute those advocating the new faith. Inquisitors vigorously hunted

down heretics, who were summarily tried, convicted, and burned at the stake or hanged.

Some nobles protested Philip's crusade, repelled by its brutality or concerned by the encroachment on provincial autonomy. Among the most vocal opponents was William of Orange, a devout Catholic and stadholder of the three northern provinces of Holland, Zeeland, and Utrecht, who like some others refused to enforce Philip's edicts in his territories. William voiced his misgivings to Margaret of Parma, Philip's half sister and regent to the Netherlands and the Council of State, an advisory board to the king: "However strongly I am attached to the Catholic religion, I cannot approve of princes attempting to rule the consciences of their subjects and wanting to rob them of the liberty of faith."

William appeared an unlikely rebel. His father, the count of Nassau in southwestern Germany, belonged to the poor branch of a noble family. When William was 11 years old, in 1544, a rich cousin died in battle in France, bequeathing him vast properties in the Netherlands as well as the principality of Orange, some 38,000 acres east of France's Rhone River. Suddenly, the boy was one of the wealthiest people in all of Europe. Charles V took him under his wing and raised him at his imperial court in Brussels as a Catholic, even though William's parents had converted to Lutheranism.

This child of fortune grew into a man of keen intellect and gregarious social propensities. William had a gift for dealing with people of all classes, and he could do it in five different languages, including French, which was the official language of the Netherlands, as well as Dutch, the common tongue. He took

great delight in falconry and in entertaining at his several palaces, his parties featuring such grand touches as wine flowing from the courtyard fountains and dishes fashioned of transparent sugar.

William's break with Philip II occurred gradually, for he considered himself a loyal servant of the king. His resentment of the monarch's attempts to suppress religious freedom was strengthened in 1561, when, after the death of his first wife, he married a Lutheran, Anna of Saxony—daughter of Maurice, who had turned against the empire. The relationship between the prince and the king worsened as Philip sought ever more

The cream of the Netherlands' nobility celebrate the 1565 nuptials of regent Margaret of Parma's son at a ball. The costly wedding festivities, which also included banquets and tournaments, antagonized commoners and gave disaffected aristocrats a chance to share confidences about their growing antipathy toward Philip II.

political power in the Netherlands, circumventing the local government at every turn. William warned the Spanish king and his supporters that they were "spinning a rope to hang themselves."

By March 1566, revolt in the Netherlands appeared imminent. On March 29, Margaret of Parma called a meeting of the Council of State and asked William to use his influence to stave off the rebellion. Reluctant to see the country descend into civil disorder, he agreed to do so if some moderate plan of government could be put in place. "In all things there must be order, but it must be of such a kind as is possible to observe," he stated. "To see a man burnt for doing as he thought right, harms the people, for this is a matter of conscience."

A week later, some 200 members of the lesser nobility, including William's younger brother Count Louis of Nassau, presented a petition to the regent that demanded the suspension of the heresy edicts and of the Inquisition. One of her ministers urged Margaret not to be afraid of this "troop of beggars." But Margaret, fearing complete loss of aristocratic support, reluctantly agreed to suspend the harsher measures of Philip's policy until a delegation could be sent to Spain to explain the situation. Her delighted petitioners proudly adopted the name Beggars and even had medallions cast showing Philip II on one side and on the other, two hands clasped over a leather bag, an item carried by many beggars along with a wooden bowl. Margaret's unexpected concession marked the beginning of a turbulent 12 months.

In various cities, attendance at Catholic services plummeted. Em-

Daughter of Charles V, Margaret of Parma grew up in Flanders, married the duke of Florence in 1536, at age 14, and briefly assumed administration of that city after his murder in 1537. She soon wed the duke of Parma, in northern Italy, where she remained until appointed Netherlands regent in 1559, one of several 16th-century Hapsburg women to govern there.

boldened by the Beggars and Margaret's apparent moderation, Calvinists who had been banned from the cities began returning and congregating openly. On Sundays, thousands streamed into the countryside for services in open fields, referred to as "hedge preaching." Armed escorts accompanied the preachers, who claimed their lives had been threatened, and other attendees also came bearing pistols, pikes, swords, and pitchforks.

Magistrates warned people that such illegal assemblies were punishable by death, but to no effect. In Antwerp, indignant crowds, hearing rumors that government troops were being sent to disperse the meetings, gathered outside the town hall to protest. When local officials tried to break up the gathering, the crowds shouted, "We want the prince of Orange!"

The regent sent an urgent letter to William, asking him to go to Antwerp to pacify the people, so early in July, he left his pregnant wife to travel there. As William well knew, the turbulence in Antwerp and elsewhere was heightened by economic hardship. Declining trade, partly the result of Philip's harsh policies and partly the result of English competition in the textile industry, had led to unemployment and idle hands in a land that had been for many years the center of European trade and manufacturing. Grain prices fluctuated unpredictably, making food costly. Margaret urged the prince to handle the situation ruthlessly. Instead, he instituted a program of public works to employ the jobless. He also urged the Calvinists to stop attending services armed and indicated that he was making plans to allow them to worship inside the city. Soon he was able to write the regent that everything in Antwerp was calm.

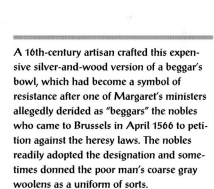

It was the quiet before the storm. On August 2 a government adviser wrote a friend in Spain that towns in the Low Countries were in turmoil. "It is to be feared that the first blow will fall on the monasteries and clergy and that the fire, once lit, will spread." And so it did. During August the Calvinist fervor sweeping the Netherlands reached a stunning climax. Starting in west Flanders and spreading rapidly to Antwerp (the day after William departed for Brussels) and throughout the 17 provinces, bands of zealots invaded Catholic churches. They destroyed stained-glass windows, statues, altars, paintings, books, vestments, chalices of silver and gold, crosses—everything that smacked of idolatry. This iconoclastic fury—the *beeldenstorm,* in Dutch—resulted in the sacking of 400 churches and convents in west Flanders alone. Bizarre scenes of destruction such as

A 16th-century artisan crafted this expensive silver-and-wood version of a beggar's bowl, which had become a symbol of resistance after one of Margaret's ministers allegedly derided as "beggars" the nobles who came to Brussels in April 1566 to petition against the heresy laws. The nobles readily adopted the designation and sometimes donned the poor man's coarse gray woolens as a uniform of sorts.

the beheading of statues in Ghent by mere children while authorities watched helplessly became commonplace.

In Madrid, when Philip II heard of the beeldenstorm, he was beside himself with fury. He tore at his beard and cried, "It shall cost them dear!" While Philip developed plans for punishing the Netherlanders, Margaret of Parma worked desperately to buy time to organize her own counterattack against the Calvinists. In late August, at the height of the riots, she met again with the minor nobility—the Beggars—and agreed to permit freedom of worship where it already existed.

The religious excesses of August turned some who had supported political protests back to the regent's side. In October William arranged a meeting with one of the Netherlands' leading nobles, Count Egmont, a stadholder and respected soldier whose support

Protestants attend open-air sermons outside Antwerp *(above),* emboldened by the Beggars' opposition to Philip's religious policies. Margaret's inability to stop the "hedge preaching," which occurred all across the Low Countries, encouraged long-oppressed Calvinists to vent their fury against Catholic churches, wrecking statues, smashing windows, ripping vestments, and slashing altarpieces *(right).*

for any stand against Philip would be important. They and a few other noblemen met in a small hunting lodge in east Flanders. William drew Egmont off into the kitchen for a private word, and there, perched on a butcher block, the prince of Orange tried urgently to win the count over. Egmont refused. William shook his head. "Alas, Count Egmont," he said, "you and your like are building the bridge for the Spaniard to cross over into our country."

In the following months, William did what he could to calm fears in the three provinces of which he was stadholder, ironing out difficulties between the old and new religions. He succeeded fairly well, but his path of moderation would not be followed long. Philip's army of 10,000 mostly Spanish troops, led by his ablest general, the 60-year-old duke of Alva, was on its way. By

February 1567 Margaret felt confident enough to demand that all the leading ministers swear a new loyalty oath. Egmont and many others acquiesced; William refused. Meanwhile, the prince of Orange was selling off jewelry and other valuable items and sending the money to his family's home in Germany.

William was in Antwerp in March 1567 when word reached him that a band of armed rebels had been attacked just outside the city by government troops. William had ordered the gates closed, but 2,000 citizens forced their way out, determined to help fight the attackers. William jumped on his horse and rode in pursuit. "You run but on your deaths," he cried as he pulled up before the angry mob, "their cavalry will kill you." His obvious sincerity persuaded them, and they returned to the city. It was a

bittersweet victory, however, for William knew that too soon the fighting would be upon them all.

As reluctantly as Antwerp's citizens had turned back, so did William of Orange make his own retreat. On April 10 he sent his resignation to Philip and prepared to leave the Netherlands. A crowd of bewildered citizens followed him to the city gates, demanding to know where he was going. "To Dillenburg for the hawking season," he replied. And with that half-truth he left.

Alva arrived and set upon a reign of terror. Margaret was dismissed. The duke, an austere and authoritarian veteran who detested heresy, wrote the king, "There is a new world to be created here." To create it by punishing those deemed responsible for the Calvinist uprising, he established a special court officially called the Council of Troubles but known to the people as the Council of Blood.

such a purpose was being smuggled out to him from several well-to-do Netherlanders. Using those funds, together with the remains of his own fortune, William was able to hire German mercenaries in 1568 to invade the Netherlands. But he and his brother Louis, who led separate armies, were quickly crushed by Alva and forced to retreat.

By 1572, at age 40, William's situation seemed hopeless. Nearly penniless, he was being hounded by creditors. The Spanish had taken over all his possessions in the Netherlands. William's marriage was in shreds. Anna, who had been indulged all her life, did not take kindly to penurious life in exile. Given to uncontrollable moods and outbursts, she drank too much and finally ran off with a married lawyer, a refugee from Antwerp. In the face of such public and private failure, William showed a firm inner

"Expect no surrender so long as I remain alive."

For more than six years, the Netherlands suffered under Alva. Thousands were arrested, thrown in jail, and tortured. Property was seized, executions carried out. Egmont, who had refused to join William's cause, nonetheless was executed in 1568 for his earlier protests of some of Philip's policies. People were sometimes condemned en masse, in groups as large as 40 or 50. Alva's spies and informers were everywhere; emigration was now forbidden. Wrote an English visitor in Antwerp, "Now the very Papists do perceive that the Duke of Alva doth go about to make them all slaves."

From his ancestral home in Germany, William poured out a series of pamphlets denouncing the Spanish occupation. Though he was unsuccessful in persuading the Protestant princes of Germany to assist him in raising an army, money for

resolve. "Exert yourself to the utmost, however hopeless the situation," he once said, "and persevere even when all attempts have been unsuccessful."

Naval raids provided William with an unexpected source of revenue. They were the work of a motley crew of ill-disciplined and fiercely anti-Catholic disgruntled noblemen, dispossessed merchants, unemployed fishermen, and assorted ruffians known as the Sea Beggars. Their 30 ships were weather-beaten merchantmen bearing secondhand cannon nailed to rotting decks under torn and patched sails. William's brother Louis had originally organized the Sea Beggars to aid in the 1568 invasion. After the attack failed, they plied the English Channel preying upon Spanish shipping and plundering the Dutch coast. This practice had a certain legitimacy, since they carried commissions from

William, who was the focus of opposition to the Spanish tyranny. As the sovereign of the principality of Orange, a tiny enclave in southeastern France, William could issue so-called letters of marque permitting the bearers to seize merchant ships of another nation. Operating out of the friendly southern ports of England, the Sea Beggars soon turned into indiscriminate pirates, asking alms from ships of all nations through the mouths of their cannon. In March 1572 England's Queen Elizabeth, not yet ready to risk offending Spain, banned the Beggars from her ports.

On April 1, 1572, desperate for food and other provisions, the Sea Beggars sailed into the port of The Brill, hometown of one of their captains, at the southwestern tip of the province of Holland. To their relieved surprise, no Spanish troops protected this small coastal town. Triumphant and exhilarated, the Beggars took possession in the name of the prince of Orange, plundered the Catholic churches, and proclaimed that everyone would be well treated "except priests, monks and papists."

The beachhead at The Brill caught William by surprise; he had planned another campaign, but not this soon. Conditions were ripe for revolt, however. Popular discontent focused on the so-called Tenth Penny, a 10 percent tax on every commercial transaction, imposed by the duke of Alva to finance his army of occupation. Opposition to the Tenth Penny was so fierce that in Brussels, bakers, brewers, and butchers had simply ceased trading to avoid paying it. After the Sea Beggars seized The Brill and fanned out to neighboring ports, town after town rose up against the Spanish.

William's own plans for military action during 1572 largely hinged upon help from the Huguenots, the French Protestants with whom he had been cultivating relations. His brother Louis invaded the southern Netherlands from France with a small force of them in May. In August, after three months of desperately raising money to pay his German mercenaries, William led an army of some 16,000 into the southern province of Brabant. But there would be no further help from the Huguenots. The king of France suddenly turned on them, ordering a massacre that doomed William's hopes. Louis surrendered in Sep-

Though finely dressed in this portrait, William of Orange had to sell much of his wardrobe to help fund his revolt against Philip II of Spain. Here he has on a black velvet skullcap, which he sometimes wore to cover his thinning hair.

tember. William himself barely escaped capture by the enemy one night when his white pug dog roused him by yapping indignantly and then jumping on his head. William eventually fled north to his old province of Holland, a rebel stronghold. He intended to "maintain the cause there as far as that may be possible," he wrote his brother John, "having decided to make my grave there."

Reinstalled as stadholder by the local councils in Holland and Zeeland, William assumed formal direction of the revolt. Though he soon converted to Calvinism, he retained his tolerance for all forms of Christianity. His aim, he said, was "to restore the entire fatherland in its old liberty and prosperity out of the clutches of the Spanish vultures and wolves."

At first, William struggled to sustain the rebels' resolve despite a series of severe setbacks. Alva ordered the slaughter of residents in three former rebel towns—Mechelen, Zutphen, and Naarden. During the summer of 1573, he besieged the northern Holland town of Haarlem, which capitulated after seven months. Then, at the end of October 1573, Alva put the revolt to its most crucial test. He launched the siege of Leiden, another Holland city, which had about 15,000 inhabitants and stood 10 miles inland among rich pastures reclaimed from the North Sea.

The first phase of Alva's siege lasted nearly five months and had relatively little effect on Leiden. In late March 1574, the Spanish troops pulled back eastward to meet an invasion of 15,000 German mercenaries led by William's brother Louis, who had rejoined the fray. The Spanish forces, superior in number and quality, crushed the invasion in mid-April, killing both Louis and his 24-year-old brother Henry. William, who already had sacrificed so much, now had lost not only two of his top commanders but "mine own brethren, whom I loved more than mine own life."

In late May William and his government faced a renewed siege of Leiden. Nearly 10,000 Spanish-led troops returned to man and fortify the 62 redoubts encircling the town. They did not intend to actually attack Leiden but simply to starve it out. This was a real possibility because the town had neglected William's advice to lay in adequate stores of food and weapons before the siege was resumed. Now it was difficult even to get messengers into Leiden, and William resorted to carrier pigeon to communicate. Hold out for at least three months, he urged the citizenry, and he would devise the means of their deliverance. William, more than anyone, realized that he had to save Leiden. One more major setback might cause the entire revolt to collapse.

BRIELE.

On April 1, 1572, the Sea Beggars take the town of The Brill, Holland, to gain the Dutch revolt's first toehold in the Netherlands. The rebels happened to attack when the port's Spanish troops were deployed elsewhere and most of its male residents were out fishing. A false report that the approaching Beggar forces numbered 5,000 men prompted most of The Brill's remaining citizens to flee.

The prince of Orange was not an outstanding general on the battlefield—no match certainly for the duke of Alva—but he had a gift for strategic planning. He knew his people were better sailors than soldiers. Why not, he asked, let the sea re-claim the land in front of the town? In that way, his little navy could sail across the flooded pastures and relieve Leiden. To carry out this radical scheme, the coastal dikes protecting the town would have to be cut and the great river sluices opened. It would be a great sacrifice, for the salt water would destroy the harvest and the fertility of the fields. He persuaded Holland's legislative body to approve his plan and even to guarantee reimbursement for the farmers. To help finance the scheme, Holland's ladies of substance donated their silver, jewelry, and costly furniture.

Early in August, William traveled to the village of Capelle for the cutting of the first of 16 breaches in the dikes along the IJssel and Meuse Rivers. Then a week later, he fell ill, worn down by his personal and public burdens. "My head is so dazed with the great multitude of my affairs that I scarcely know what I am doing," he wrote his surviving brother, John. He lay gaunt and feverish in a former convent in Rotterdam. To ease the stifling heat in the bare room, servants laid green branches on the floor and sprinkled them with fresh water. Still his fever soared, and rumors of his death spread quickly.

Even in his worsening condition, William knew he could count on the courage and patriotism of the chief magistrate of Leiden. Adriaen van der Werff was a former tanner and dealer in chamois skins who had been banished from the Netherlands for his ardent Calvinism in 1566. In exile, he had won William's confidence by carrying out secret missions into the Netherlands. Now, in the besieged city, he presided over a local government that enforced rationing, protected the vegetable gardens that produced some cabbages and turnips, and guarded the few cows and horses left grazing under the city walls.

In late August, van der Werff's spirits lifted. A carrier pigeon arrived with a letter of reassurance from William, dictated from his sickbed. The dikes had been pierced, the prince announced, and the water was rising. To rally morale, van der Werff had the letter read in the marketplace and cannon fired to signal receipt of the good news. At his orders, the city's musicians marched around the town, along the lovely tree-shaded canals and over the stone bridges spanning them, playing lively melodies and rousing martial airs. The cannon flare lighted up the sky and the music drifted over the walls, astonishing the Spanish troops.

By the time William was up and about in early September, his flotilla for relief of Leiden was ready, crewed by more than 2,000 sailors—many of them scarred veterans of the Sea Beggars. Some 200 flat-bottomed barges propelled by oars and poles were assembled and mounted with cannon or laden with provisions.

The flotilla got off to a good start. Water flowing through the broken dikes was deep enough for the vessels to sail unimpeded to a point about five miles from Leiden. Spanish troops there guarded a two-foot-high dike, the outermost of three barriers protecting the town from the sea. The Beggars broke through on the night of September 10, but then progress stalled. Skirmishing with the retreating Spanish defenders and repeatedly bogging down in the mud, the vessels moved only two or three miles during the next three weeks. The water finally became so shallow that the sailors could see cattle grazing in the meadows in the approaches to Leiden.

The boats stood stranded in nine inches of water. They needed twice that depth to float. William was rowed out to the motionless armada to give the crews a pep talk, but inwardly, he was not optimistic. He had known that the combination of strong wind and high tide necessary to push sufficient torrents of water through the broken dikes was unlikely at this time of year. By carrier pigeon he sent off one last message of reassurance to the citizens of Leiden, scarcely more than two miles away.

The situation was desperate in the city. There had been no bread for more than a month, and the malt cake that replaced it was gone. The last horses and cows were being slaughtered. People were eating rats and stripping green leaves from the trees. On top of the hunger, an epidemic of plague had descended upon the populace. Thousands were dead or dying. Van der Werff awoke one morning to find a corpse in front of his door. It had been

Starving Leideners greedily devour bread and herring tossed from the vessels of the Beggars' relief flotilla, which had sailed straight into the city across land that had been flooded by William's forces. Some long-suffering townsfolk choked to death in their haste to eat.

placed there as a protest against his repeated refusals to negotiate surrender with the Spanish commander. When an angry crowd gathered around him in the center of town, he lashed back. "Here is my sword," he told them, "plunge it into my breast, and divide my flesh among you. Take my body to appease your hunger, but expect no surrender so long as I remain alive."

On the night of October 1, the event that William had thought improbable happened. A violent gale coincided with high tide. The North Sea piled over the dikes and rushed inland. In 24 hours, the stranded Dutch armada lifted on two feet of water and sailed toward Leiden. At one fortified village, the Spanish launched a few vessels of their own, and the cannon fire of a strange little naval engagement lit up the orchards. The Dutch pushed on and, at dawn on Sunday, October 3, 1574, found that the Spanish defenders had marched away in the waist-deep water. (Later, it would be discovered that the Spanish commander, unable to bear the thought that anyone should think him afraid of William's Beggars, had left a note in a nearby fort: "Farewell state, farewell little forts, who art abandoned on account of the waters not on account of the force of the enemy.") Within minutes, the sailors were at the wharves of Leiden, tossing loaves of bread to citizens so emaciated they could scarcely stand.

That Sunday, William was in church in the city of Delft, some 10 miles to the south, when a messenger arrived with the news. Against the entreaties of friends who feared he could not stand to breathe the noxious air of a city filled with pestilence, he insisted on rushing to Leiden the next day. There, he lauded a people still feasting on eggs, sausages, and cheese for their courage and endurance—and stayed long enough to make certain enough provisions were brought in to feed the town for two years.

The relief of Leiden was a turning point. No longer did William and his rebels fear a quick suppression of their revolt. During the following few years, in fact, William's vision of a united and free Netherlands, north and south, seemed realizable.

This war and the one with the Turks were such a financial drain on Spain that its troops in the Netherlands mutinied over lack of pay. In 1576 all 17 provinces signed an agreement to cooperate in ousting Spanish forces. Attempting to energize the revolt in the south, William moved his headquarters to Brussels and then to Antwerp.

William's renewed display of physical and mental energy was due in no small part to his third marriage. In a modest ceremony in 1575, he had married 30-year-old Charlotte of Bourbon, who had no dowry and had been disowned by her father, a French prince, after she fled the Catholic convent where she was the abbess and converted to Calvinism. Charlotte cared for William and his children and bore him six more, all daughters, in seven years.

Charlotte greatly feared for William's safety. Despite the fact that many Netherlanders remained loyal to Spain and detested the revolt, William appeared in public without taking precautions. In 1580 Philip II finally concluded that the only way to end the revolt was to get rid of William. Calling the prince "the chief disturber of the whole state of Christendom," the king put an enormous price on William's head.

Two years later, Juan Jaureguy, a clerk working for a Portuguese merchant in Antwerp, managed to get his pistol so close to William's face that when he fired, the prince's beard and hair were singed as the bullet passed through both of his cheeks. For nearly five weeks William hovered near death, Charlotte constantly at his bedside. Then, just as he began to recover, an exhausted Charlotte fell ill and died.

William could not hold the southern provinces, and by 1584 he was forced to abandon his dream of a united Netherlands, returning north to Delft to take up quarters in an old convent. Security there was lax, and a 27-year-old cabinetmaker's apprentice pretending to be the son of a Calvinist martyr had no trouble worming his way into the prince's confidence. Balthazar

A 16th-century engraving depicts the events involved in William of Orange's murder in Delft on July 10, 1584. At top right, William rises from a meal with his family in the dining hall of their mansion. Outside the hall, Balthazar Gérard shoots the prince, using a pistol bought with money William had given the assassin after he had claimed to be penniless. At left, Gérard makes his escape from the house but is captured before he can scale the garden wall.

Gérard was, in fact, a fanatical French Catholic who, when he was only age 12—long before King Philip's bounty—had vowed to kill William. On July 10, just outside the dining room of the prince's quarters, Gérard aimed his pistol directly at William's chest and fired twice. The 51-year-old leader staggered forward and uttered his last words, "My God, have pity on my soul and this poor people." Gérard was caught and tortured to death, but his family was able to collect the reward from the Spanish government.

Within hours of the assassination, the governing council of Holland vowed to continue the struggle that, with the help of William's son Maurice, would lead finally to permanent independence for the seven northern provinces and to peace with Spain in 1648. William's own role in that triumph was recognized by the inscription on the tomb over his grave. "Father of the Fatherland," it read, "who valued the fortunes of the Netherlands above his own."

The World's Marketplace

"Here is Antwerp itself changed into Amsterdam," marveled a visitor to the Dutch Republic's teeming port on the Zuider Zee in 1594. When Antwerp, formerly the "most renowned merchandizing City that ever was in the World," fell to the Spanish in 1585, its scepter passed to Amsterdam, which grew rich and powerful as Europe's center of commerce.

Their farmland always in danger of flooding, the Dutch were accustomed to importing many necessities. Superior ships, expert seamanship, and an entrepreneurial spirit also aided their phenomenal success as middlemen in a global trading network. The Dutch began overseas trading in the 1400s, importing grain from the Baltic and timber from Norway. Expanding their traffic to include high-value goods, such as silver and spices, they soon dominated European markets.

A tremendous boon to Dutch shipping was the invention of the cargo ship called the *fluit*, its broad-bottomed hull designed to carry a greater volume of goods. Inexpensive to build, fluits also required smaller crews. Foreign competitors often chartered Dutch ships, because they were more cost efficient than their own.

Immigrants flocked to the United Provinces, which was known for its religious toleration. The wealthy brought capital to invest in overseas trade, land improvement programs, and the profitable Dutch industries of shipbuilding and textiles. Skilled artisans introduced new crafts, such as diamond cutting and glassblowing, and unskilled day workers provided labor for new industries. The successful Dutch East India Company attracted adventurous seamen as well as risk-taking investors; its shares were a major source of speculation in Amsterdam's stock exchange.

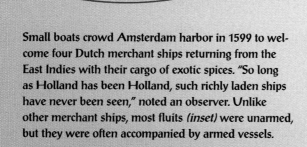

Small boats crowd Amsterdam harbor in 1599 to welcome four Dutch merchant ships returning from the East Indies with their cargo of exotic spices. "So long as Holland has been Holland, such richly laden ships have never been seen," noted an observer. Unlike other merchant ships, most fluits *(inset)* were unarmed, but they were often accompanied by armed vessels.

Lush, fertile, and flat, the countryside resembles a patchwork quilt in this painting of polders in Holland. With windmills in the distance, cattle graze, farmers talk and work their fields, and sailboats ferry people up and down the narrow canals that crisscross the landscape. In the foreground, details from a painting by Pieter Brueghel the Younger show peasants gathering and cutting grain.

Working the Land

It was often said that "God created the world, but the Dutchman made Holland." Indeed, diking as well as other drainage methods designed to keep the sea from flooding fields and towns had been employed in the low-lying Netherlands for centuries. During the 16th and the 17th centuries, however, an infusion of capital from urban investors along with advances in engineering resulted in vast amounts of additional agricultural land being reclaimed from the sea—nearly 200,000 acres in the 50-year period between 1590 and 1640.

Windmill power, already used for grinding grain and sawing timber, was redeployed, in a stroke of technological genius, to drain water from diked areas. Workers first enclosed an expanse of shallow water with a dike, then ringed the dike with a canal. The windmills, erected in a stepped array with each one on higher ground than the last, scooped the water from the enclosure in their waterwheels, passing it from one mill to the next. The water drained first into the outlying canal and then into a river or the sea. The reclaimed acres, which were still surrounded by dikes, were known as polders, and they provided fertile fields for food crops, as well as grass needed for the increasingly profitable cattle-raising industry. Dairy cattle provided many valuable commodities—milk, cheese, and butter—both for the Dutch and for export to France, Germany, and the Baltic states. Cattle also provided much-needed manure to fertilize land used continuously for agricultural produce. Other reclaimed land was set aside for growing crops that would provide the raw materials necessary to supply Holland's industries, such as flax for producing linen, hemp for ropemaking, and barley and hops for brewing beer.

Wealth from the Sea

Many Dutch looked to the water for their livelihoods. Though both fresh- and saltwater fish were abundant, Dutch fishermen grew rich on the herring trade, calling it *Groote Visscherij*, or "great fishery." The Dutch herring fleet dominated the shoals along the British coast throughout the 1500s, and by 1600, envious foreigners estimated the fleet's size at 450 boats.

Each year from June until September Dutch seamen set out in their large vessels (*buizen*, or "buses," as the English called them), to live at sea for months at a time, gathering herring that were migrating from the Baltic to the North Sea. The crew salted and packed the fish in barrels on board ship, and smaller boats shuttled provisions out and carried the fish back to port. The Dutch used herring as a form of currency, trading it in Germany for luxury goods, throughout southwestern Europe for wine and salt, and in the Baltic for grain.

In 1612 the Dutch began whaling—a profitable but dangerous business—in the waters around Greenland and the Arctic island of Spitsbergen. The Northern Company, formed by nine Dutch shipowners, won exclusive rights to the Arctic whaling grounds and, once there, edged out English competition. Whale products were in great demand: Oil made from blubber was used in soapmaking and lighting, and the flexible whalebone was used for knife handles, picture frames, and umbrellas. Because whaling was possible only in the warmer months, Northern Company employees maintained a frantic pace each summer, living and working on the whaling ships or on Spitsbergen, stripping whale carcasses and boiling blubber.

Northern Company employees prepare to slaughter a whale, which had been harpooned at sea and towed by ships to the company's camp on Spitsbergen Island. The desolation of the area only helped to emphasize the remoteness and isolation of working on a whaling ship for months at a time.

Dockworkers add salt to piles of herring in this lively 17th-century harbor scene. Salting the catch was a two-step process: Herring salted and packed on board tended to condense and settle, so the barrels were no longer full when they reached port. After salting them a second time, workers repacked the barrels to capacity.

Urban markets offered an array of fresh fish for customers such as this discerning Dutch mistress, shown pointing to her selection (left). An onlooker watches with interest as the fishmonger wields his knife, turning whole fish into choice fillets.

An Overseas Trading Empire

East India Company merchant ships and an Indian vessel fly the Dutch flag as they approach the company's trading depot on the Hooghly River in Bengal, India. Within their well-fortified walls, company officials oversee Indian workers loading and unloading crates in rows of warehouses.

Hoping to seize the lucrative Asian spice trade from their Portuguese and Spanish rivals, Dutch shipowners formed companies to finance expeditions to the Far East during the late 16th century. In 1602 the republic's States-General merged the competing companies into the Dutch East India Company, granting the conglomerate a trade monopoly east of Africa's Cape of Good Hope. Headquartered in Batavia on the island of Java, the company grew rich and powerful. Expanding its interests into textiles, porcelain, as well as other luxuries over the following century, the company remained the republic's greatest source of colonial wealth for close to 200 years.

The Dutch West India Company was less successful, however. In the 1620s it settled a fur-trading colony on North America's Manhattan Island, only to lose New Amsterdam to the English 40 years later. Beginning in the 1630s, the company played a large role in the Atlantic slave trade, transporting Africans to Brazil and the Caribbean to harvest sugarcane. After driving the Portuguese from Pernambuco in northern Brazil, the Dutch settled into colonialism there, living on sugar plantations until 1654, when the Portuguese regained their foothold.

Slaves perform back-breaking work in this painting of a Brazilian sugar mill. Workers turn a sugarcane press *(background, right)*, forcing the sweet liquid from harvested cane, while others refine the liquid by boiling it in large kettles *(foreground)*. Cane juice formed the base for rum and molasses as well as sugar.

Europe's Financial Center

With Amsterdam a hub of international trade, foreign merchants conducting business there needed a place to exchange the many coins and currencies circulating at the time. In 1609 the Amsterdam Exchange Bank *(Wisselbank)* was established, replacing private cashiers who charged exorbitant fees for their services. Businessmen could open accounts, deposit and transfer money, and exchange it for local currency.

Although the actual trading of goods like Polish grain, Brazilian sugar, or French wine took place in nearby warehouses, the financial transactions—negotiating, speculating, or buying and selling shares in profitable businesses such as the Dutch East India Company—were conducted at the stock exchange. Shops on the second floor of the elegant building on Amsterdam's waterfront sold luxury items, while below, traders from all over the world gathered around the stone pillars lining the central courtyard, making deals.

Amsterdam's leading citizens demonstrated their pride in the city's institutions by posing for formal group portraits; the one at left depicts officers of Amsterdam's coopers guild. Appointed by public officials, guild officers served as the governing body for the city's industries.

Wealthy and small investors alike could buy, sell, and speculate under the arches or in the sunny courtyard of the building known as the Bourse, housing Amsterdam's stock exchange *(above)*. Some speculators employed spies to gather inside information or spread rumors to influence exchange rates.

CHAPTER THREE

Amsterdam, the "Golden Swamp"

A 17th-century Dutch-woman plays a small piano-like instrument called a virginal, surrounded by other trappings of affluence: a gilt mirror, black-and-white marble floors, an Oriental carpet, and rich bed hangings. In the United Provinces, the 1600s were a time when trade brought prosperity, art and science flourished, and Amsterdam became one of the greatest cities in the world.

ometime between dusk and dawn, in the darkest gloom of night, a blinding shaft of light sliced through the sky, illuminating a rough stone tomb. A winged figure materialized amid the radiance and, reaching downward with supernatural strength, ripped back the heavy lid. Roman guards patrolling nearby fell back in terror, a sword flying from one man's numbed hand. From the tomb's shadowy depths, a shrouded man began to rise.

For a moment, tax collector Johannes Wtenbogaert could have imagined himself at the Holy Sepulcher 1,600 years before, witnessing Christ's Resurrection—rather than simply contemplating a painting in an Amsterdam studio on January 27, 1639. But the smell of half-dry canvases and resin-soaked rags beckoned him back to the present, and he turned his gaze from the picture to its creator. The artist presented a sharp contrast to his exquisite work, the features of his wide face somewhat coarse, the nose bulbous. A pair of intense and piercing eyes peered out from beneath a head of dark, unruly hair. But it was his talent, not his appearance, that mattered. Although the United Provinces (the seven Netherland provinces that had won independence from Spain) was home to thousands of artists, few on earth could paint images as powerful as those created by Rembrandt van Rijn.

Rembrandt's works graced the walls of the Dutch Republic's most important families. His patrons included regents—members of the rich merchant clans that controlled the commerce and politics of Amsterdam—as well as courtiers who served the prince and princess of Orange at The Hague (de facto seat of the Dutch government). Frederick Henry, prince of Orange and stadholder of five of the provinces since 1625, was Rembrandt's grandest patron, and it was he who had commissioned the picture of *The Resurrection of Christ* and its companion piece, *The Entombment*. His Highness, already the proud possessor of three paintings on the subject of Christ's Passion, was eagerly awaiting the two pieces that would complete the series. Rembrandt had promised speedy delivery of these works—three years ago.

The artist had attempted to excuse the lengthy delay in a letter sent to the prince's secretary, Constantijn Huygens, 15 days earlier. Announcing that the pictures had been finished, "through studious application," Rembrandt continued: "In these two pictures the greatest and most natural emotion has been expressed, which is also the main reason why they have taken so long to execute." The truth, however, was that the painter had been busy with other projects, and only the recent purchase of a new house had spurred him to finally deliver on his promise to the prince.

Rembrandt's future home was a tall, handsome house on the Breestraat (where many other painters and publishers as well as the city's burgeoning Jewish community lived), and the price was as impressive as the architecture—13,000 guilders. The artist had signed an agreement to hand over the first 1,200 guilders on May 1, with another 2,050 due before the same date in 1640, and the remainder payable within five or six years' time. There would be interest due as well. This sum was far in excess of the amount that most prosperous Dutch burghers would have spent on a new home, about 1,900 guilders. But Rembrandt undoubtedly felt he deserved a residence appropriate to his status.

To obtain the necessary funds, Rembrandt had hurriedly completed *The Resurrection* and *The Entombment*. So eager was the artist to collect his money that he had not even allowed the pictures to dry completely before readying them for delivery. He had, in fact, been in the midst of packing them when Wtenbogaert had come knocking at the door.

The artist did not always welcome visitors to his studio. As contemporary Italian art historian Filippo Baldinucci would recall, "When Rembrandt was at work, he would not have granted an audience to the first monarch in the world, who would have had to return again and again until he found him no longer engaged." But Wtenbogaert had come with a generous financial offer for his friend. The tax collector knew that Rembrandt was eager to receive his money as soon as Frederick Henry signaled his approval. But he also knew that Volbergen, the prince's paymaster in Amsterdam, tended to treat funds passing through his hands as if they were his own. If Volbergen thought he could get away with it, he would keep Rembrandt waiting months or even years for his fee. If it pleased the prince of Orange, Wtenbogaert would make the payments from his Amsterdam office as a matter of convenience to both parties. The prince could then pay the tax collector.

Rembrandt thanked Wtenbogaert and soon showed him out. After he finished packing the two paintings, the artist scribbled another note to Huygens, mentioning the tax collector's offer. "Therefore I would request you my lord that . . . I may receive this money here as soon as possible, which would at the moment be particularly convenient to me." As a postscript he added: "My lord, hang this piece in a strong light and so that one can stand at a distance from it. Then it will show at its best."

As his overly packed schedule of commissions clearly showed, Rembrandt had done well for himself in Amsterdam over the past seven years. He had moved there in late 1631 from his hometown of Leiden, one of the thousands of newcomers who had been flocking to the republic's most prosperous and powerful city in recent decades. In 1600 the population had numbered 60,000; by 1639, it had risen to 135,000 residents. One person in every four was foreign.

Expanding to absorb the burgeoning population was no mean feat for a settlement that was little more than a cluster of islands in a swamp. Engineers drove wooden pilings—as huge as the masts of the seafarers' ships—deep into the underlying mud and silt to provide a solid base for new buildings. (To underpin a single building, the new town hall, 13,659 pilings would be ordered in 1648.) Wrote scholar and poet Caspar Barlaeus of this phenomenon, "I consider it no small thing that I have moved to a city that floats amid swamps and marshes, where the burden of so many buildings is held up by forests of wooden pilings, and where decaying pines support the most prosperous mercantile center in Europe."

Amsterdam's air was full of sawdust and the sound of hammering. Three new semicircular canals, lined with handsome houses for the mercantile elite, cut through the fan-shaped metropolis. New quays accommodated the ever more numerous ships; new warehouses sheltered their cargoes; new bridges, gates, and walls controlled the flow of foot, wheeled, and floating traffic. On the city's landward edges, gardens and meadows vanished under the march of the carpenters, stonemasons, and bricklayers.

People from all walks of life moved to Amster-

Along the Bowmen's Bastion moat, one of Amsterdam's many urban waterways, rise the homes of the well-to-do, including twin mansions built behind a single neoclassical facade *(right)* for the Trip brothers, whose family patronized Rembrandt. Mortar-shaped chimneys and decorative cannon in the gable reflect the Trips' arms trade.

dam, their reasons numerous. Artists such as Rembrandt went because the city was a flourishing scene for culture and the arts as well as a center for business, government, and learning. Caspar Barlaeus, who like Rembrandt had come from Leiden in 1631, migrated to help establish the Athenaeum Illustre, predecessor to the University of Amsterdam. Some people were drawn by careers and service to the new Dutch Republic. Others came eager to enlist in one of the republic's two great colonial enterprises and seek their fortunes overseas. Many would prosper in the city Constantijn Huygens called "the golden swamp," but others would flounder. Rembrandt would do both, achieving greatness but losing a fortune.

Born in Leiden on July 15, 1606, Rembrandt was the second youngest of at least nine children born to a prosperous miller and his wife, whose family were bakers. Rembrandt's father was a Calvinist and his mother a Catholic, a sign of the religious tolerance that was to be found in the United Provinces.

Having impressed his parents with his intelligence, a seven-year-old Rembrandt was sent to Leiden's Latin School, to be prepared for entrance to the University of Leiden and a learned profession. The curriculum included Latin, the classics, and Calvinist religious studies. At age 14, Rembrandt was enrolled at the university but left after only a few months to pursue art.

Following a three-year apprenticeship with a Leiden painter, Rembrandt traveled to Amsterdam, where for six months he was taught by one of the republic's foremost artists,

Rembrandt's wife Saskia perches on the knee of her boisterous husband in this portrait the artist painted around 1636. A pigeon pie on the table awaits them. On the wall at the upper left hangs a tally plank, a board on which innkeepers kept track of how many drinks each customer had ordered.

Pieter Lastman. From Lastman, who had studied in Italy, Rembrandt learned superior drawing techniques and chiaroscuro, the interplay of light and shade in a picture. Chiaroscuro would become his central stylistic principle, and he would wield it with a skill unsurpassed by others to achieve a deeply dramatic effect. The artist also developed a great interest in historical paintings, particularly those with biblical themes, perhaps a result of his Calvinist upbringing and deepening spirituality.

Back in Leiden, Rembrandt set himself up as an independent artist, creating paintings, etchings, and drawings. He quickly made a name for himself in his hometown and attracted a handful of students, an indication of just how much his work was respected.

It was in his hometown, in 1629, that the miller's son met Constantijn Huygens, who had commissioned a painting from another local artist, Jan Lievens. Rembrandt often worked closely with Lievens,

cousin Saskia, the orphaned daughter of a distinguished politician from the province of Friesland.

They became engaged in June 1633; Rembrandt was almost 27, Saskia not quite 21. Three days after the betrothal he drew a portrait of his future bride in silverpoint on a costly sheet of white vellum; she wore a wide-brimmed straw hat trimmed with flowers and held a flower in her hand. The look in Saskia's lively eyes, captured so vividly in the drawing, made it clear that this was a love match as well as one of material and social advantage for the groom.

Rembrandt had already established himself as a master of his trade, who had sold historical and biblical scenes, mythological and genre paintings, portraits, and other works to collectors back home in Leiden and in The Hague. In Amsterdam he had swiftly carved out a place as the most successful portraitist in the city, able to charge top

"Because you are naked you must get out of Paradise!"

the two men sometimes retouching each other's paintings. Huygens admired the work of both artists and urged them to go to Italy for further study. They did not have time, the two men replied, and besides, they could see Italian paintings in the Netherlands. But Rembrandt's chance meeting with Huygens still proved fortunate, for almost certainly it was through Huygens that the artist received his first commissions from the prince of Orange.

By 1631, Rembrandt had decided Leiden could not adequately support him as an artist and moved to Amsterdam. His first residence there was in the home of art dealer Hendrik Uylenburgh, whom he had met while in Leiden. Not long after his arrival, Rembrandt was introduced to Hendrik's pretty young

prices for his likenesses of local dignitaries. But he was still a humble miller's son; his alliance with Saskia, however, lifted him several rungs up the social ladder. Her family circle included lawyers, a professor, a town clerk, and an army officer; her friends came from the class of affluent burghers who could well afford to purchase Rembrandt's art.

On June 22, 1634, Rembrandt and Saskia were married in a church in the Friesland town where one of her sisters lived. Most Dutch weddings occurred either in the Reformed church with a preacher or in the town hall, where a local magistrate officiated. If the newlyweds followed custom, they then led a procession of their friends and family back to the house where they were staying, while flowers were tossed upon them.

Besides giving her husband access to potential patrons, Saskia came into the marriage with some money of her own. The couple would come to need those funds, for neither Saskia nor Rembrandt was particularly frugal, and the exotic wares that crammed the city's shops offered all too many temptations. The couple's free-spending habits eventually caused Saskia's relatives to accuse them of frittering away her inheritance "with ostentation and display." Rembrandt would never learn how to manage his financial affairs to his own best advantage, but he worked tirelessly at his trade. By the late 1630s business seemed better than ever. He was a successful member of a thriving industry whose products were always in demand.

Dutch householders, whatever their station in life, had a seemingly insatiable appetite for all kinds of artworks. Foreign travelers, such as the Englishman John Evelyn, found this characteristic fascinating: "Pictures are very common here, there being scarce an ordinary tradesman whose house is not decorated with them." Peasants and laborers bought the artwork from itinerant artists who set up booths at fairs and markets to sell their modestly priced drawings, prints, and paintings. Scenes of tavern and army life, depictions of mischievous maidservants and children at play, as well as biblical and moral images were always popular.

Prosperous burghers sought to fill every foot of blank wall space with evocative landscapes, elegantly composed still lifes, or peaceful domestic interiors. The purchase of art, like the acquisition of good furniture, was regarded as an entirely permissible form of conspicuous consumption: What could be more virtuous than the beautification of the

Pupils in a Netherlands painting academy practice drawing the human form *(above)*. Earlier in their apprenticeship they would have learned how to grind pigment, mix paint, lace canvases onto stretchers, and prepare copperplates for engraving or etching. At right, potential buyers visit an artist's studio to view finished pieces and works in progress.

family home? To seek out the most pleasing works, they might buy directly from an artist, patronize a dealer, or place a bid at an auction.

The wealthiest Hollanders could, like Prince Frederick Henry, commission original works on themes of their own choosing. They sat for individual portraits or posed proudly with fellow members of various civic bodies. Rembrandt painted group portraits that ranged from the officers of the Clothmakers Guild to the Militia Company of Captain Frans Banning Cocq, the latter becoming known to posterity under the title of *The Night Watch*. But the person he painted most often, with a mirror carefully positioned near his easel, was himself. At first exercises in capturing different facial expressions, his self-portraits may eventually have become a means of recording the journey from young man to old. He would create at least 90 such portraits, more than any other artist.

Rembrandt's expensive new house on the Breestraat, to which he and Saskia moved on May 1, 1639, gave him plenty of room and excellent conditions in which to work. His studio was a large, airy space occupying the whole of one story of the house. The white-walled room was lighted by four high north-facing windows, equipped with external and internal shutters that could be adjusted to achieve the precise amount and angle of illumination required.

To supplement his income, Rembrandt attended auctions and bought artworks for resale. In 1638, he had invested in eight separate sets of Albrecht Dürer's woodcuts on the life of the Virgin Mary; he may have planned to keep one set for himself, but the rest would be passed on, at a price, to a dealer or to private customers of his own.

As in Leiden, Rembrandt also earned money through teaching. Young hopefuls—and some older, more experienced artists who knew a master when they saw one—paid him an annual fee of 100 guilders each. He drew or painted alongside them, or walked among them as they worked, guiding a novice's awkward hand, sketching out a solution to a technical problem, suggesting some simple alteration that turned a mundane effort into a piece worth framing. He also offered his disciples the opportunity, still rare, of drawing from live models.

In a warehouse he had rented to accommodate his many students, Rembrandt set up small cubicles, walled with paper or canvas, where the artists could work without distraction. But he may have regretted this arrangement when, on a sultry summer afternoon, he arrived in the studio to find his pupils, consumed with fits of giggles, trying to peer into a gap between two partitions.

The First Museums: Collectors' Cabinets

Guests in the home of a prosperous 17th-century Netherlander would probably be taken on a tour of their host's collector's cabinet, an international collection of art and artifacts like the one shown at right. The typical cabinet of a merchant or an aspiring courtier might occupy one room; wealthy collectors filled multiple rooms within their capacious homes.

The collections reflect the Dutch interest in probing the world's mysteries and ranged from natural wonders to exotic wares. A burgher might own Japanese lacquerware, an elephant's tail, tobacco pipes, coins, and insects with gilded wings. Every inch of open wall space would be adorned with paintings of contemporary Dutch and Flemish artists such as Rubens, Rembrandt, Jan Vermeer, and Anthony van Dyck. Originals often hung next to copies of the same painting.

Anatomist Frederik Ruysch filled at least five rooms of his house in Amsterdam with a collection of rarities—skeletons, human organs, and other *naturalia*. He had engravings made of them for future scholars to study. Another Dutch collector modestly said of his cabinet: "I present to you herewith the Almighty Finger of God . . . by his Spirit and Grace, which He has bestowed on mankind, that they can investigate these high and hidden wonders and for the benefit of other men display the same."

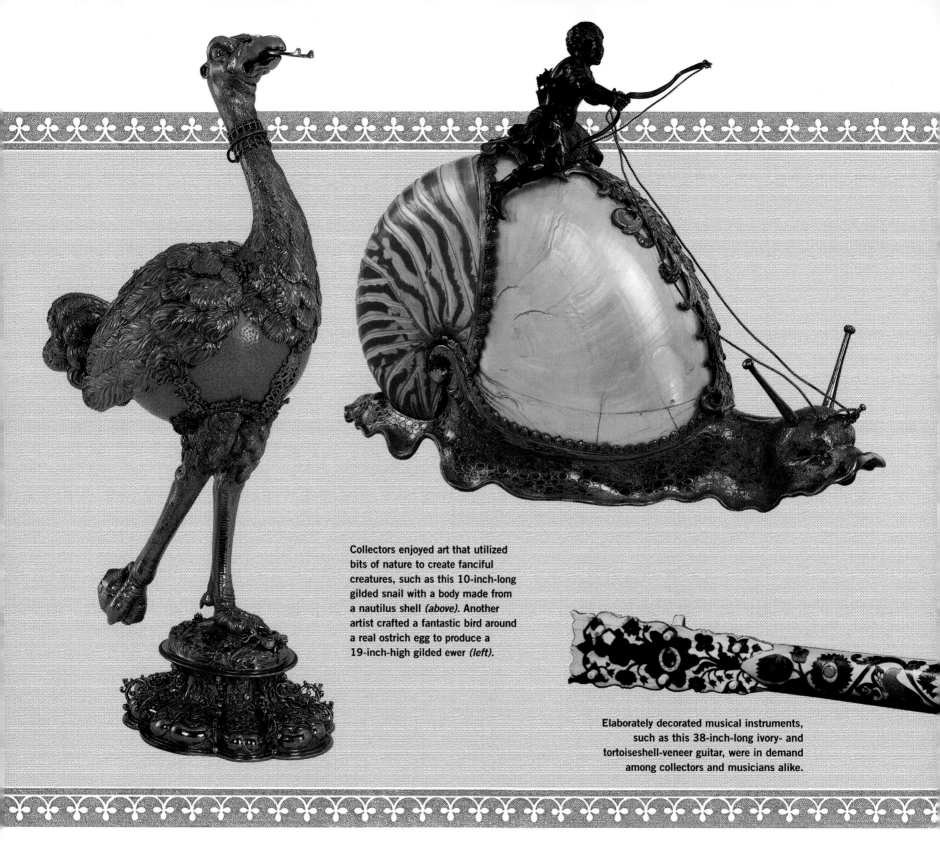

Collectors enjoyed art that utilized
bits of nature to create fanciful
creatures, such as this 10-inch-long
gilded snail with a body made from
a nautilus shell *(above)*. Another
artist crafted a fantastic bird around
a real ostrich egg to produce a
19-inch-high gilded ewer *(left)*.

Elaborately decorated musical instruments,
such as this 38-inch-long ivory- and
tortoiseshell-veneer guitar, were in demand
among collectors and musicians alike.

The first Dutch travelers to meet the Chinese emperor in the 1650s brought back stories of their wondrous journeys to the East, spurring an avid interest in jade, porcelain, and lacquerware like the Ming dynasty dish at left, carved with dragons.

Designed to be both utilitarian and beautiful, this 24-inch-tall compound microscope is covered in vellum and stamped with gold. Scientific and humanist study fascinated collectors, who reveled in examining the miniature world captured under the glass of a microscope.

The Dutch, fascinated by the Roman Empire, eagerly acquired coins such as this one bearing the likeness of Emperor Julian.

119

While drawing a nude model, one young cutup had apparently decided to keep her company by removing his own clothes.

Startled by their teacher's sudden appearance, the pack of Peeping Toms fell silent. In that moment of stillness, the young man's voice rang out, "Now we are naked like Adam and Eve in Paradise."

Rembrandt promptly banged on the wall with his stick, yelling, "Because you are naked you must get out of Paradise!" Then he rushed in and chased the pair out of the studio. Tripping and stumbling, they struggled to get themselves back into their clothes as he harried them down the steep staircase and out into the street.

To recover his equilibrium after this unsettling little drama, Rembrandt may have gathered up his sketchbook, pens, and ink and set off for a walk in the summer sunshine. Even as he strolled through the city, Rembrandt never stopped working. For years the artist had filled his ever present sketchbooks with vivid moments of city life, captured swiftly on the spot and transformed at leisure into etchings: an elephant from a traveling circus; two butchers at work on a pair of carcasses; a pancake vendor luring customers with the buttery smell and sizzle of her hot, fresh wares.

Seeking a different world, Rembrandt also ventured into the countryside. Here too he found a wealth of subject matter: a man in a rowboat, a tumble-down cottage with grass growing out of its roof tiles, a boundary stone, a windmill, the dreamy ruins of an old fortified house called Kostverloren.

Occasionally he paid a visit to his country-dwelling friend Jan Six, who lived on the Diemerdijk waterway. At Six's house, Rembrandt drew his host writing at a window and made an etching of a nearby bridge, with two men in tall hats leaning peacefully on the railing and contemplating the boats on the river.

As well as providing inspiration, these long walks may have offered some distraction from his domestic woes. In June 1642, just eight years after their wedding, Saskia died. She left Rembrandt with their nine-month-old son, Titus. At some point after his wife's death, Rembrandt began cohabiting with the motherless baby's nursemaid. Geertge Dircx was a short, stocky peasant woman from northern Holland, who had entered the artist's service after the death of her husband, a trumpeter in the town of Hoorn. Rembrandt gave her some of his late wife's jewelry, including a costly ring set with diamonds. When Saskia's relatives heard of this gift they were appalled, though they might have been reassured to learn that Dircx, in a will she made during a spell of illness in 1648, explicitly bequeathed the jewels to Saskia's little boy. Perhaps she did so at Rembrandt's insistence or perhaps she simply considered herself Titus's new mother as well as Rembrandt's common-law wife.

The relationship between the artist and the nursemaid came to an ugly end. By 1649 there was another woman, one Hendrickje Stoffels, living in the Breestraat house. Dircx demanded a financial settlement as the price for her departure. When negotiations broke down, she sued. What was the ring, she demanded, if not a pledge of their betrothal? On September 25 of that year, Rembrandt was summoned to a hearing by the Commissioners of Marital Affairs and Damage Claims. With seeming indifference, he declined to appear, sending Stoffels to submit a deposition in his place.

By this time he nursed a grievance of his own. Dircx, having lost her home at the Breestraat, was finding life expensive in her rented room. To Rembrandt's horror, she began to pawn some of Saskia's jewels. Even after the court ordered the artist to pay her maintenance—200 guilders a year for the rest of her life— Dircx persisted in her trips to the pawnshop.

Their wranglings came to an end in 1650. Rembrandt appears to have entered into a conspiracy with

Dircx's brother and cousin, who hoped to claim her money for their own. Their maneuverings, which may have included a smear campaign to brand her as a woman of irredeemably loose morals, led to her confinement at the House of Correction in the town of Gouda. Rembrandt himself paid the 140 guilders due for these proceedings and pressed the officials to sentence her to a full 12 years' detention.

A group of Dircx's female friends and relations, finding out about her situation the following year, took up her cause. In May 1655 one of them arrived at the Breestraat. She announced that she was on her way to Gouda to have Dircx released. Rembrandt, spluttering with fury, jabbed his finger at her face and warned, "If you go, you will regret it." His threats proved useless. After five years' imprisonment, Dircx was freed. She went home to her native province of Waterland, putting as much distance as she could between herself and her former paramour. With Dircx out

of the way, Rembrandt settled into a long relationship—a marriage in all but name—with Hendrickje Stoffels.

As both a lover and an artist, he found her serene face and sensuous figure irresistible. Rembrandt painted and drew her over and over again—dozing in a chair, standing at a window, lifting her shift above her thighs as she waded into a river to bathe. He crowned her with a garland of flowers and transformed her, as he had Saskia, into a personification of the goddess Flora. In 1654 she posed in the nude for his painting of *Bathsheba with King David's Letter.*

This very public display of Stoffels's obvious charms may have been one cause of the troubles that beset her in that year. Many of the women who served as artists' models were prostitutes. In Amsterdam's brothels, nude paintings of the courtesans were displayed so customers could make their choices. Most people felt no respectable Dutchwoman would allow herself to be painted

without her clothes on. Thus despite the fact that Stoffels and Rembrandt had by this time enjoyed some five years of unwedded bliss, the elders of the Reformed church now ordered Stoffels to appear before their council on a charge that "she practiced whoredom with Rembrandt the painter."

Such a summons was fairly routine. Although officials knew many cases of fornication were not reported, whenever such an incident came to their attention, they vigorously pursued the people involved. Their object was to break up illicit affairs and to bring the offenders to repentance and reform.

Stoffels ignored three council summonses before finally appearing before the group on July 23 and admitting to her relationship with the artist. It would have been hard to deny it, since she was six months pregnant at the time. The councilors ordered her to repent her sins and denied her the right to take Communion. For many church members, such punishment was devastat-

ing. Not only were their reputations damaged, but their souls were endangered as well.

Respectability and Communion rights might be regained by leading a repentant and unblemished life under the eyes of a local preacher for several years, but this course held no appeal for Stoffels. Not even the loss of her connection with the church—which would be permanent—persuaded her to give up Rembrandt. Three months later she gave birth to a daughter, named Cornelia after the artist's mother.

Despite the birth, Rembrandt did not marry Hendrickje Stoffels. He may have been put off by the terms of Saskia's will, which would have forced him to hand back her money to the van Uylenburghs if he remarried and Titus, Rembrandt and Saskia's son, subsequently died. This proviso was not the only deterrent. Hendrickje was the daughter of an army sergeant, so her origins were as lowly as Dircx's. The painter may have started life as the

On Amsterdam's IJ, a sea inlet, people mingle on the ice for business and pleasure, some in outdoor garb, others wearing indoor clothing over layers of woolens. At far left, a man draws a fishing net up through a hole in the ice; nearby, someone has erected a tent, from which he or she may be selling drinks. In the right foreground, two men play the Dutch game of *kolf*. Horse-drawn sleds and armchairs on runners provide transport for those too young or old to skate.

son of a floury-handed miller, but he now considered himself a gentleman. A wife such as Stoffels, no matter how much he loved her, could jeopardize that hard-won status.

But Rembrandt soon found himself driven out of this carefully constructed Eden. He had done everything he could to make himself a proper bourgeois—marrying a wellborn lady, buying a handsome residence, and furnishing it with costly objects in the best contemporary taste. But he had committed a fatal error, one that no true Holland burgher could forgive: He bungled his financial affairs. He invested unwisely, lived beyond his means, and plunged ever further into debt in a vain effort to pay off the mortgage on his house.

In 1656 Rembrandt admitted defeat and had himself declared insolvent. His worldly goods were inventoried and sold off to satisfy his creditors—antiques, furniture, Oriental *objets d'art,* porcelain figurines, and the 70 paintings and hundreds of drawings and etchings that still remained in his possession. Eventually the Breestraat house was sold.

To satisfy the rules governing Rembrandt's artists guild, all of his commercial operations now had to be conducted through other parties. Stoffels and Titus—by this time in his late teens— set themselves up as art dealers. Rembrandt became their employee, providing advice about purchases and supplying them with his own works for sale. In spite of these reverses, Rembrandt's creative juices never ran dry: He would produce some of his greatest works in the years between his fall from bourgeois grace and his death in 1669.

In 1663, the 39-year-old Stoffels, after what seems to have been a long period of decline, died. Though Titus assumed control of the art dealership, at age 22 he was still a minor (in the Dutch Republic, males and females were considered minors until age 25). Two years later, Rembrandt supported his son's petition to the States-General to allow his legal status as an adult so he could better run his business.

Rembrandt's son married in 1668 but lived only another seven months before succumbing to illness. Rembrandt would die the following year. One of his final pieces of art was a self-portrait, showing a man with a face lined by age and suffering but whose dark eyes still looked out upon the world with an artist's curiosity.

On a summer day in 1635, some three and a half years after Rembrandt first moved to Amsterdam, another young man traveled to the port in search of a new life. Twenty-two-year-old German Stephan Carl Behaim's reasons for the journey were quite different from the artist's. He had come, supposedly, to join a ship's crew of the Dutch East or West India Companies. The companies drew adventurers from all over western Europe, some joining in hopes of winning wealth and glory, others simply keen on escaping debt collectors or the gallows. The East India Company required its new employees to sign up for seven years' service; the West demanded four.

Behaim's relatives back home in Germany had been happy to see him depart. "This hopeless scamp," lamented his half brother Lucas Friederich in a letter to another kinsman, "frequented inns and other dark corners, gambled, caroused and raised hell. The money we entrusted him for legitimate expenses he maliciously spent on other things." A brief career as an army courier had come to an inglorious end: Behaim had disobeyed orders by riding alone through a dangerous district and had to surrender both his horse and his mailbag to a gang of bandits. Upon his return, Behaim was promptly thrown in the brig for a few months.

His half brother, not knowing what else to do with a young man who squandered every opportunity and did not hesitate to lie and cheat, wrote a family friend in Amsterdam, Abraham de Braa, asking for help in finding Behaim a place with one of the trading companies. De Braa informed Friederich that ships left only a few times a year for the East and West Indies and Brazil, but if Behaim could be persuaded to enlist, "I will gladly do my part to help him in this. . . . [and] can advise him on how to keep his expenses at a minimum." Unfortunately, the last thing Stephan Behaim cared about was keeping his expenses in check.

"I have always borrowed money with extreme reluctance, sadness, and inconvenience to myself," proclaimed Behaim on August 21, 1635, in an outrageous letter home. He was, the young man vehemently declared to his long-suffering mother, "for sure and without any doubt making the supreme effort never again in my life to be a burden." After this pronouncement, Behaim got to the point of his missive, the usual one: He

TULIPOMANIA

Rembrandt was not alone in making unwise investments. In the mid-1630s, the Dutch passions for gambling and tulips converged, and speculation in bulbs pushed prices up so high that a masterly still life like the one at left cost far less than the flowers portrayed. This "tulipomania" occurred only a few decades after the flower had made its way to the republic from Turkey. At first the preserve of aristocrats and botanists, tulip growing quickly spread as nursery owners began publishing illustrated catalogs and sending salespeople to villages and fairs to hawk the bulbs.

Development of new varieties further whetted collectors' appetites. The most sought-after flowers sported red-and-white or purple-and-white flamed or feathered patterns—actually the result of a virus, a fact then unknown. By 1636, the willingness of enthusiasts to pay an amount equal to the cost of a town house for a single bulb of a prized variety encouraged speculators from all walks of life to enter the market. In between the planting of the bulbs in October and their lifting, or removal for transplanting, in June, ownership of a bulb might change hands several times, with its price increasing daily and even hourly at the height of the frenzy. The tulip futures market came crashing down in February 1637, when the government stepped in to curb what had become known, due to its ephemeral nature, as the "wind trade."

needed funds. "I could earn not a little traveling money, if I had twenty thaler to invest here in cheap goods to take with me to the West Indies."

But Behaim's money—or rather his family's—was not going for anything so practical. As in Germany, he was finding it difficult to resist the pleasures to be found around him. Amsterdam, the town of respectable burghers and merchants, also offered much in the way of entertainment for young men of Behaim's character.

Taverns ranged from luxuriously appointed hostelries where army officers and burghers toasted each other in crystal goblets of Mosel wine to plebeian drinking dens

Revelers at an inn dance to a tune played by a bagpiper *(foreground)* and her fellow musicians. By the early 17th century, Amsterdam had one alehouse for every 200 inhabitants; Dutchmen from all ranks of society, as well as many lower-class women and even children, avidly patronized these establishments.

awash with beer and reeking of cheap tobacco. It was easy to find a table full of companions ready for a card game or a shake of the dice, favorite pastimes of Behaim's despite a typical statement about personal reform in another letter home. In explaining that the company's wages should cover most of his expenses, he declared: "This does not include unexpected losses from gambling, a pastime I have renounced anyway."

For lovers of wine, women, and song, and Behaim was surely among them, the favorite resort was the *musico,* a drinking hall equipped with a small orchestra—often of wretched quality—and a bevy of professionally friendly females who would never refuse a customer's invitation to dance. Local prostitutes used the musicos as a base of operations; the authorities tended to turn a blind eye upon the trade as long as it remained discreet.

Official tolerance stopped short whenever rowdiness and lewd behavior spilled onto the streets. Women prosecuted for drunkenness, prostitution, brothel keeping, or theft were commonly sentenced to a term in the city's spinning house. The inmates of this establishment were put to work spinning, knitting, or sewing garments for the city's orphanages while their warders read to them from pious texts.

Confinement did not mean isolation. The public was allowed in to watch the women at work, and the spinning house became a popular stop on 17th-century Amsterdam's tourist trail. English, German, and Italian visitors were intrigued to observe these "incorrigible and lewd women" bent over their needlework or spinning wheels like diligent housewives.

However full the spinning house, Behaim found no shortage of cheerful and available young women to put their arms around his neck, teach him the latest bawdy songs, and help him spend his money. He reveled his way through approximately two and a half guilders a day. It would have taken a clergyman or scholar three years to earn the sum that trickled through Behaim's fingers during his six months in Amsterdam.

Finally, through de Braa's intervention, Behaim was recruited into the West India Company as a musketeer. The company needed all the experienced soldiers it could find to fight off the Portuguese threats to its Brazilian colony. This offer of a post came not a moment too soon, Behaim confided to de Braa; a pack of creditors were nipping at the young German's heels.

On November 24, 1635, the day Behaim was to report to his ship, de Braa set off with some servants to fetch the recruit from his lodgings. Though the Dutchman had formed a good understanding of Behaim's character by this time, he was shocked to discover that the young man had disappeared into the city. Only 12 days before, de Braa had signed Behaim with the company, paid off the keeper of the young German's boardinghouse (where he had been allowed to run up an extravagant bill), and installed him in a more modest establishment. But Behaim had taken only one meal in the new lodgings before departing.

After de Braa searched frantically through Amsterdam, someone in a tavern or a musico must have tipped him off about Behaim's whereabouts. The Dutchman discovered that his charge was in hiding at his old boardinghouse. "He was at the time looking for every excuse to get out of the voyage (which he had never taken seriously)," wrote de Braa to Lucas Friederich. But after all his pains, de Braa was not about to let Behaim wriggle out of his grasp. He and a servant stood watch while the recruit packed up his things, then virtually frogmarched him to West India House to receive his musket and two months' advance wages. Once de Braa made sure that Behaim was safely on board the good ship *Harlem,* he breathed a sigh of relief and sent the family a bill to cover his considerable expenses. He also assured them: "If his family would like to see him remain in Brazil for a longer time, the means can be found here to arrange that he must."

De Braa's prayers of thanks were premature. The West India Company convoy lay becalmed in the harbor of Texel for several weeks, waiting for a good wind. Although living on board ship,

Behaim was able to disembark, go shopping, and get himself even deeper in debt. He had already spent one of de Braa's many cash advances on new body linen and extra food. Not wanting to lose de Braa as a future monetary source, Behaim wrote home asking that the man be promptly reimbursed for the various expenditures.

Behaim reminded another of his suppliers, a cousin of de Braa's, that he owned only two suits of outer clothing. One was a green summer suit in a light, thin fabric, ideal for Brazil's hot climate. But the weather in Texel was "constant bitter cold"; Behaim had been forced to bundle himself up in both suits, wearing them night and day. So the green coat, doublet, and trousers were now, said Behaim, "worthless." According to his comrades, new clothes cost a fortune in Brazil. Surely it would be only sensible for him to buy what he needed before leaving Holland?

Whatever the outcome of this particular request for supplies, the young German's attempts to garner more funds and provisions were temporarily suspended when a good east wind finally filled the *Harlem*'s sails. The 66-day voyage, Behaim later wrote, was blessed by "beautiful weather all the way from England. We saw many marvelous fish, whales and flying fish among others." But when he stepped ashore in Pernambuco, the recruit soon realized that his troubles had crossed the Atlantic with him.

Nothing seemed to go right. Whatever funds Behaim received, whatever help he was given by the countrymen he met in Brazil, money and success still slipped through his fingers. Although dazzled by the tropical flora and fauna—"the enrapturing vegetation, animals, and birds which God has bestowed on this land"—he concluded that life in Brazil brought only hardship, debt, and disappointments.

Behaim's letters to Germany became as querulous and as riddled with excuses as those he had sent from Amsterdam. Then suddenly they stopped. In April 1639 Lucas Friederich wrote to de Braa: He had heard nothing from his brother in a year and a half. Had any word of him come to Amsterdam?

De Braa wrote back with bad news. Caspar Stör, a German officer in one of the West India Company regiments, had seen Behaim in November 1637 at Fort San Francisco. The musketeer was in a terrible state. He was dirty, demoralized, half-crazed with fever, clad only in a tattered coat. His lack of any shoes or stockings revealed a hideous injury, possibly received in battle or on the march: A rotting, half-severed toe dangled from one foot. Every step he took was agony.

Appalled, Stör had his compatriot carried off to the garrison hospital in Recife. The place was filthy and the care rudimentary, but Stör could not think of any alternative. He was about to leave the district on a military mission, but he promised Behaim that he would visit as soon as he could. When, after a year's absence, he managed to get back to Recife, Stör learned that Behaim had died of blood poisoning in January 1638. His last letter home, on May 14, 1637, had been a request for money.

While Stephan Behaim lay dying half a world away from Europe in a filthy, reeking garrison hospital, medical knowledge in the United Provinces was making significant advances, moving the Dutch to the forefront of the field. Rather than relying on speculative theories alone, research was being performed to learn more about the human body and how it functioned, primarily by means of human dissection. Public anatomies were performed annually in Amsterdam and throughout western Europe—in Padua, London, and other centers of learning—from the end of the 15th century until well into the 1800s. No conscientious medical man would have missed them: In London, a 1572 ordinance decreed that even foreign doctors who happened to be visiting the English capital had to attend or pay a fine.

Public anatomies were

A windmill dominates a riverbank landscape along a branch of the Lower Rhine, not far from Utrecht. Sailboats and passenger barges plied Dutch waterways on regular schedules, linking towns in an intricate and affordable transportation network. Some busy barge lines, such as the one between Amsterdam and Gouda, even provided night service.

conducted only in the coldest months, to ensure that the body stayed in good condition until the work was done. Evenings were preferred to daytimes; daylight was less dependable than the steady, artificial glow of lamplight.

On a January day in 1632, just after Rembrandt had moved from Leiden to Amsterdam and three and a half years before Stephan Behaim arrived there, the cream of Amsterdam's surgical and medical fraternity filed solemnly into the city's spotless anatomy theater. Illuminated by a chandelier with at least a dozen tapers or lanterns, the chamber, most likely located in the old weigh house at St. Anthony's Gate, was filling up rapidly. Not only were medical practitioners in attendance, but the black-clad burghers—magis-

the center of the room. Upon it, naked except for a white cloth draped over the loins, lay the corpse of a man named Adriaan Adriaanszoon—better known to his friends and enemies as "Aris the Kid." Adriaanszoon—convicted of robbery, assault, and at least one attempted murder—had been hanged the previous day.

Dissections were appreciated by the wider community as a delightful mixture of instruction and entertainment. Those who relished the spectacle of criminals receiving their due on the gallows could enjoy the subsequent dissection of their corpses as a final act in the drama of public punishment. For avid churchgoers, an anatomy was almost as good as a sermon, full of lessons about sin, mortality, and retribution. At this particular performance, the presiding

"Cut and cut deep, and you will find the source of the problem."

trates, clergymen, scholars, and merchants—as well as ordinary men, women, and children and a good sprinkling of foreign visitors could also be seen. The amphitheater's front-row seats were reserved, according to rank and seniority, for the members of the surgeons guild; tonight they were joined by Rembrandt, who would be making preparatory sketches for a painting that had been commissioned to commemorate the event. At his back, packed close together on rising tiers of benches, sat the burghers.

The treasurer of the surgeons guild could feel a quiet glow of satisfaction as he counted the house. Apart from official guests, each member of the audience had paid seven stuyvers for a ticket. Tonight would certainly bring in at least 200 florins, enough to cover costs, pay for the feast and torchlight procession that traditionally followed, and still make the guild a decent profit.

The focus of everyone's attention was the revolving table in

physician was Nicolaes Tulp. Of the 50 or 60 practitioners working in Amsterdam at the time, few if any were as well qualified to conduct the forthcoming procedure. In keeping with the new experimental spirit of the age, Tulp believed that pathology—the study of the origin, nature, and course of a disease—was "the very eye of medicine," the key to understanding both the workings of the human body and the dynamics of the illnesses that undermined it. Dissection was an essential tool in that study.

"Cut and cut deep," Tulp urged his fellow practitioners, "and you will find the source of the problem." In addition to the public anatomy lessons, Tulp pursued his scientific investigations in more private and less theatrical environments, using corpses from the hospitals run by the city as shelters for the sick and homeless poor. That night, Tulp held center stage; when all eyes were upon him, he began the procedure.

In Rembrandt's *The Anatomy Lesson,* members of the surgeons guild listen intently to Nicolaes Tulp during his dissection of Adriaan Adriaanszoon. Tulp's talent as an anatomical lecturer was celebrated not only by painters but also by at least one poet, Caspar Barlaeus. "Here, while with artful hand he slits the pallid limbs, speaks to us the eloquence of learned Tulp: 'Listener, learn yourself! and while you proceed through the parts, believe that, even in the smallest, God lies hid.' "

Although only 39 years old at the time, Tulp had already established himself as one of the leaders of his profession. He was the son of a local cloth merchant but, instead of following his father's trade, had studied medicine in Leiden under the tutelage of the most distinguished physician of the day.

His family and friends called him by the name he had been christened with—Claes Pieterszoon—but he conducted his professional and public life as Nicolaes Tulp, or "tulip." This flower, prized by the Dutch above all others, became his personal trademark: He had it carved into the gable of his stately house on the Keizersgracht (one of the grand new semicircular canals) and incorporated it into the coat of arms that adorned his carriage. Tulp was the first physician in the city to use a coach to speed his way to a patient's bedside.

In 1641, nine years after he had been

immortalized by Rembrandt, Tulp published an account of his most interesting clinical cases. Some of the illnesses he treated were lodged in the mind rather than the body. He described the delusions suffered by Caspar Barlaeus, "the greatest orator and poet of our age," who believed that his hindquarters were made of glass and feared to sit down in case they shattered.

Another patient, a talented painter whose name Tulp did not divulge, conceived the notion that his bones were melting and dissolving. Dreading the moment when his legs would buckle under him, the artist took to his bed in a state of profound depression, staying under the covers for an entire winter. Not until the spring could Tulp convince the man that his fears were groundless.

Tulp and his like-minded contemporaries brought a breath of fresh air into a profession that still took many of its theories from medieval apothecary texts—and whose members had not yet entirely abandoned such magical remedies as bird droppings collected when the moon was full. He was in the vanguard of a new generation of Dutch clinicians who kept in touch with current developments in physics and chemistry, valued the experimental process, and emphasized the importance of cleanliness and hygiene in the prevention and treatment of disease.

Wary of dubious treatments that had nothing to commend them apart from their antiquity, Tulp compiled a collection of 60 simple and practical prescriptions—he was, for instance, a great believer in the efficacy of drinking copious amounts of tea. In 1636 he persuaded his colleagues to set up the Collegium Medicum, a commission to regulate and inspect the city's 66 apothecary shops. To reduce the number of women dying in childbirth, he set up training courses for midwives.

Tulp chose as his personal emblem a burning taper accompanied by the motto, "I consume myself in the service of others." Those whom he treated came from all walks of life—patricians, shoemakers, captains of the guard, the victim of a brawl who had been stabbed so violently that his lungs were visible through the gaping wound. The doctor interested himself not only in the health of Amsterdamers' bodies, but in the welfare of their city and, as a church elder, in the salvation of their souls. As time went on, he expended more of his energy on the business of local government and less on medical matters.

The city of Amsterdam was an oligarchy governed by a tight network of wealthy families, who occupied all important public offices and sat on the commissions that governed virtually every aspect of civic life, from maritime affairs to bankruptcies to domestic squabbles. Most of these governing burghers—who were known collectively as the regents—came from old merchant or landowning families. They married each other's sisters and passed on their political power—along with their comfortable fortunes—to their heirs.

The clique occasionally opened its doors to admit new blood. In 1622 Dr. Tulp, by virtue of his professional eminence, had been welcomed into this not-quite-closed circle and invited to take up one of the 36 seats on the city council. When, after the death of his first wife, he married a lady of impeccably patrician stock, Tulp's star rose even higher. In the course of a long political career he spent eight terms as city treasurer, sat on the board of the East India Company, and was elected, four times over, to the exalted post of burgomaster.

The burgomasters, four in number, represented the uppermost tier of the city government. Officially, they were guided in their actions by their brethren in the council; in reality, however, they were answerable only to themselves. They appointed every public official, selected the members of all commissions and colleges, and wielded almost untrammeled power over all commercial, financial, legal, and religious activities.

The burgomasters' influence inevitably extended well beyond the municipal boundaries. Amsterdam was by far the richest city in the province of Holland, and Holland was the richest province of the seven that composed the Dutch Republic. In the highest councils of state, Amsterdam's representatives spoke with the loudest voices. These august bodies might convene in The Hague, but few disputed Amsterdam's position as the fountainhead of the nation's wealth and power. In 1650 Holland gained even more status when William II, Frederick Henry's successor as prince of Orange and stadholder, died of smallpox. Five of the provinces chose not to name a new stadholder, and Amsterdam's leaders grabbed the power. Foremost among them was Johan de Witt, who would direct the republic's domestic and foreign policies for almost two decades, from 1653 until 1672.

Meanwhile Tulp, as a man of strong views and firm convictions, used his own position to mold the minds—and improve the morals—of his fellow Amsterdamers. Although he was a lover of poetry and the fine arts, a devotee of literary gatherings and an enthusiastic art patron, Tulp was also a strict Calvinist. And, like other Calvinists, he felt particularly uneasy about the theater.

In the early part of the century, the city fathers almost succeeded in suppressing the theater altogether; at times the only performances permitted were those staged to raise funds for charity. The traveling companies who entertained the populace with broad comedies and gory dramas were regarded with contempt; the men of letters, such as Joost van den Vondel (the most esteemed Dutch poet of the day), who wrapped political commentary inside a thin veil of classical imagery, made the authorities nervous.

In 1637, despite some vigorous opposition from the clergy, the burgomasters had relented sufficiently to allow a permanent theater. The new stone playhouse was erected as a commercial investment by the directors of the city orphanage, which helped justify ticket sales as contributions, however indirect, to that worthy institution. The premiere performance was a drama penned by Vondel, *Gijsbrecht van Aemstel,* celebrating the glory of Amsterdam. But not even the name of Vondel would suffice to protect a play from official censorship. In 1654 Tulp and his fellow burgomasters banned the performance of Vondel's *Lucifer* after the Reformed church complained about blasphemous language.

Shortly afterward, Tulp launched a crusade against his fellow burghers' increasing enthusiasm for extravagance, luxuries, and frivolous pursuits. In the old days, as he no doubt fulminated over the plates of good plain fare at his family supper table, Amsterdam's leading inhabitants were models of simplicity, decorum, hard work, and sober tastes. But in recent years, they had begun seeking a grander lifestyle, one befitting their higher social status, forsaking their ancestral shops and counting houses for a life of leisure, acquiring titles, family trees, and country mansions.

Tulp found the current fashion for sumptuous wedding feasts particularly galling. No one disputed the right of two families to rejoice at the union of their young, but the

Seated before an almshouse she established, a Dutch benefactress oversees the distribution of grain to the elderly residents of her foundation. In Amsterdam, charitable and penal institutions, like the city's governmental departments, were supervised by members of wealthy families.

doctor felt these festivities were getting out of hand, with hundreds of guests, enough food to feed an army, enough drink to float the fleet, and brigades of musicians tootling and sawing away, day and night, until the better part of a week was squandered.

In 1655 he and a fellow burgomaster passed a law banning such excesses. It allowed a maximum of 50 guests and half a dozen musicians, set a time limit of two days for the revels, and decreed that the total value of gifts should not exceed one-twentieth of the bridal dowry. Anyone who quibbled would have been sharply reminded that such an expenditure—in addition to offending God—was unseemly in a year when Holland was scourged by a visitation of the plague, a serious economic depression, and the effects from the recently concluded naval war with England.

A primary cause of the Dutch-Anglo conflict had been trade rivalry, as the Dutch continued to prosper and control the trading routes. In 1652 England had declared war. The English, with their vastly superior navy, had won engagement after engagement, devastating the Dutch fleet and economy. During this time, the Dutch Republic had lost possession of its prosperous Brazilian colony to the Portuguese. But the English economy had suffered as well, and a peace treaty had been signed in 1654.

The free-spending rich were not the only targets of Tulp's attentions. Like his fellow Calvinists, he wished to eradicate every vestige of Roman Catholic ritual or pagan superstition. The Reformed church ministers abhorred the "papist idolatry" and "Baal worship" of such popular events as the Feast of Saint Nicholas, when the entire population regaled their children with dolls and puppets, lit candles in curious human shapes, bit the heads off gingerbread men wrapped in silver paper, put their shoes near the chimney, and awaited the visitation of Sinter Klaas, or Saint Nicholas.

On December 4, 1663, two days before the holiday, Tulp and another burgomaster persuaded the city magistrates to forbid the "idolatrous" sale of dolls, imposing a three-guilder fine on any street vendors caught flouting the ban. The regents found that they had reaped a whirlwind: The Amsterdamers and their young let out a roar of protest, then celebrated their favorite feast day in the usual manner. The magistrates wisely chose not to attempt to enforce the ban.

There was one celebration that Tulp's fellow regents deemed thoroughly justified. On January 28, 1672, they assembled at the doctor's house to mark his 50 years' membership on the city council. Tulp's friends and colleagues were determined to honor him as he deserved, even though the Dutch Republic was facing some dangerous times as another war, this one with France and England, loomed on the horizon.

In the course of nine hours—from 2:00 in the afternoon to a daringly late 11:00 p.m.—a distinguished company of patricians, medical practitioners, poets, statesmen, scholars, and other worthies toasted Tulp with the finest Burgundy, dined on a dozen separate courses, passed around dishes of blue Ming porcelain containing mounds of perfumed tobacco, and smoked their pipes as various men of letters read their verse tributes to the host.

While savoring the excellent wine, those guests of a reflective nature might have looked upon the now venerable Dr. Tulp and mused that his life was itself a mirror of their own city's rise to greatness. He had sprung from solid mercantile stock, marshaled his resources to make himself a leader in his chosen field, sought to live according to the dictates of his faith, and did not hesitate to avail himself of the earthly rewards all his talents and hard work had brought him. When they lifted their glasses in yet another salute to their host's achievements, they were hailing not only Nicolaes Tulp, but Amsterdam's own age

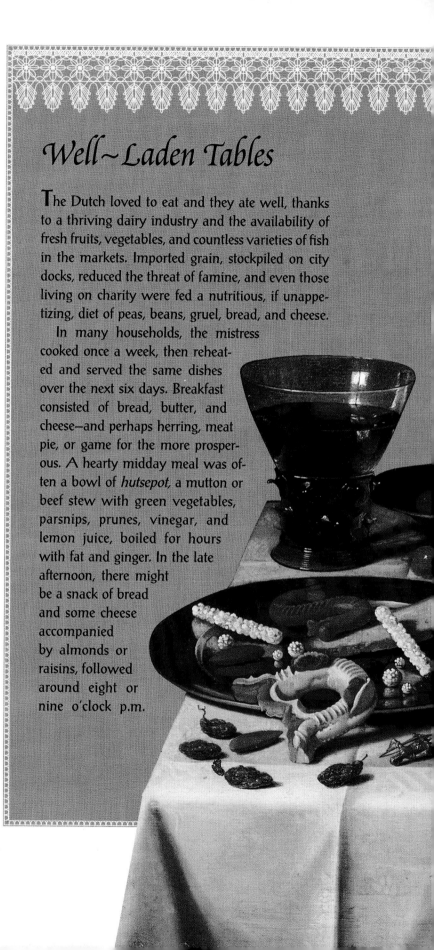

Well~Laden Tables

The Dutch loved to eat and they ate well, thanks to a thriving dairy industry and the availability of fresh fruits, vegetables, and countless varieties of fish in the markets. Imported grain, stockpiled on city docks, reduced the threat of famine, and even those living on charity were fed a nutritious, if unappetizing, diet of peas, beans, gruel, bread, and cheese.

In many households, the mistress cooked once a week, then reheated and served the same dishes over the next six days. Breakfast consisted of bread, butter, and cheese—and perhaps herring, meat pie, or game for the more prosperous. A hearty midday meal was often a bowl of *hutsepot,* a mutton or beef stew with green vegetables, parsnips, prunes, vinegar, and lemon juice, boiled for hours with fat and ginger. In the late afternoon, there might be a snack of bread and some cheese accompanied by almonds or raisins, followed around eight or nine o'clock p.m.

On a banquet table laden with culinary delights, a pie has been cut into, revealing the succulent mincemeat within. The pie is surrounded by bread, walnuts and hazel-nuts, and platters containing imported lemons, green olives, and a variety of fancy cookies. A pitcher and plates made of gleaming pewter, crystal goblets, and a finely crafted and pressed lace-edged tablecloth proclaim this a meal for a well-to-do household.

by dinner—usually the day's leftovers. Beer was consumed at every meal (most of the water was contaminated), by children as well as adults.

During the republic's golden age, the banquet tables of the wealthy groaned with lobster, oysters, fine European wines (often spiced with ginger, cinnamon, and cloves), and tea from the East Indies. And with over 50 sugar refineries operating in Amsterdam by the mid-1600s, the Dutch developed a passion for sweets such as pastries and marzipan, a staple at all feasts. Though amazed by the amount of food and drink that the Dutch consumed, foreigners were less impressed with the quality. Cooks, grumbled one visitor, boiled or roasted everything "all to Rags, so that you don't know what sort of Flesh 'tis when it come to the Table."

In the midst of preparing for a huge feast, the mistress of the house lards a hare before cooking it to tenderize the meat. The banquet table can be seen through the open doorway.

A Dutch family shares good food, fine drink, and comfortable companionship: A younger woman, her shoe resting on a foot warmer, has her wineglass refilled while the grandmother studies a music sheet and an amused father teaches his son to smoke a pipe.

of glory. Tulp's time, however, and the city's golden age were both coming to an end. The doctor lived two more years, just enough time to watch as his beloved republic plunged into yet another conflict.

In a matter of weeks after Tulp's celebration, the French and the English joined forces against the republic, attacking its trade routes and fisheries, pounding its ships with cannon fire, and blockading its ports. French and English motives for the war were rooted in events of the previous decade.

The first Dutch-Anglo war had ended in 1654, but another had erupted in the 1660s. This time a rebuilt Dutch navy emerged triumphant, and England was forced to concede shipping rights and New World colonies. (The English did hold on to New York, formerly New Amsterdam, which they had seized from the Dutch in 1664.) Meanwhile the French, who had promised to aid the republic but did so half heartedly and belatedly, invaded the Spanish Netherlands. The invaders hoped to gain territory since Spain's gradual loss of political power and its peace with France had led it to withdraw much of its military from the region. When France struck, both England and the Dutch Republic saw the move as a threat to their own sovereignty and allied temporarily in January 1668 to force French king Louis XIV to make peace with Spain.

Furious, Louis subsequently sought to undermine Dutch power and influence, entering into a secret agreement with England in June 1670 to seize Dutch territory and colonies. In the spring of 1672, England and France launched attacks by land and by sea. By July, three of the seven provinces had been lost to French troops. The remaining provincial governments of the Dutch Republic seemed ready to capitulate to the enemy. But the people themselves rose up to stop their leaders with protests and riots. In Amsterdam, the protests reached their peak in September 1672. The Amsterdam stock exchange had crashed, bringing commerce to a standstill and causing widespread financial havoc. The population, feeling the pinch, grew mutinous, and the governing class found itself riven by internal schisms.

On the military side, meanwhile, two Dutchmen in particular were responsible for holding the enemy at bay: William III and Michiel de Ruyter. The newest prince of Orange, William III, was installed as stadholder of Holland and Zeeland in July 1672 (after 22 years without any-

Several generations of a wealthy Dutch family make music together with a variety of instruments. Sing-alongs were a favorite winter activity of Dutch householders, and most homes contained several songbooks, ranging from those with religious or patriotic themes to more light-hearted collections with titles such as *Trombone of Joy* and *Little Kisses Written in Latin.*

one in that position) and subsequently declared prince-captain and admiral general of the entire republic. Admiral Michiel de Ruyter, a highly regarded naval hero, patrolled the sea and waterways. But even such men as these were not above suspicion in a time when the Dutch felt threatened on all sides.

On the afternoon of September 6, 1672, in an unpretentious section of Amsterdam filled with fishermen and sailors, Michiel de Ruyter's wife, Anna, heard angry shouting outside her door.

Only her niece and two maids were at home with her. Alarmed, she peered out a window and caught sight of a mob of hundreds of women and men bearing down on her house. Shocked and uncertain of what to do, Anna was relieved when a relative came out of his house next door to demand an explanation from the threatening crowd. De Ruyter, mob members shouted, had "betrayed and sold the country's fleet." They had heard that for money the admiral had virtually surrendered the Dutch fleet to France. De Ruyter, they had been told, had already been arrested as a traitor; someone even claimed to have seen him, bound and shackled, being marched into prison in The Hague.

Hearing her husband's reputation soiled by such lies, Anna retrieved a letter she had just received from Michiel, sent only the day before from Schooneveld, where he waited with the fleet. In it, he spoke of his hopes of engaging the enemy before long. Anna handed the missive over to the admiral's accusers. Among the crowd were people who knew Michiel de Ruyter's handwriting; they quickly verified that the letter was genuine. The mob then turned upon their leaders and denounced them as scoundrels for maligning the good name of a heroic naval leader.

Well aware that during a riot only last month, such a crowd had killed two of Amsterdam's political leaders, one of them Johan de Witt, Anna breathed a relieved sigh. She returned to the shelter of her four-story house, perhaps wondering whether it would not have been better for her family to

have stayed in their hometown of Vlissingen, Zeeland. But for better or worse, they had made the decision to move to Amsterdam 18 years ago for the sake of the Dutch Republic.

In March 1654, Michiel de Ruyter had been promoted to vice-admiral of the Amsterdam Admiralty with a mission of protecting the Dutch trading fleet against the harassment of the pirates who haunted the Mediterranean shipping lanes. Operating from bases all along the North African, or Barbary, coast, from the Strait of Gibraltar to Algiers and Tripoli, these raiders pillaged cargoes and held crew and passengers to ransom or perhaps sold them for a tidy profit in the slave markets of Italy and Spain. Michiel had declined the honor of the appointment at first, feeling a growing desire to retire and a great loyalty to his home province of Zeeland.

Born in the rough-and-ready port of Vlissingen in 1607, Michiel de Ruyter, like Stephan Behaim, had been in trouble as a boy. He had been expelled from school for misbehavior and subsequently fired from the menial job he had taken with local shipowners. But there was a significant difference between the two men: De Ruyter decided to make something of himself.

At the age of 11 de Ruyter had gone to sea for the first time, in the lowly capacity of boatswain's boy. By his early 20s he had visited the West Indies and Brazil and served as both a gunner and a cavalryman in the war between the young republic and Spain (which did not officially end until 1648). He had endured a siege, sailed with a man-of-war, suffered a dangerous head wound in a sea battle in the Bay of Biscay, and been captured by the Spanish. He had then given his jailers the slip and fled home, on foot, through France.

Ambitious for advancement, de Ruyter filled notebooks with self-taught lessons on stellar navigation, the use of the compass, and all the other arts and crafts of seamanship. He rose in the ranks of the merchant fleet, went into the North Atlantic with the Greenland whalers, and commanded his own ship on trading missions along the Barbary coast and in the West Indies.

In war and what passed for peace, his courage and resourcefulness enhanced his rep-

Michiel and Anna de Ruyter *(second and third from left)* pose with family members: her son from a previous marriage *(fourth from left)*; the three children of the admiral's second marriage, two daughters *(standing, right and center)* and a son *(far left)*; and his son-in-law *(second from right)*. Michiel and Anna's two young daughters *(front)* play with a cousin.

utation. The dockside taverns buzzed with tales of de Ruyter's triumphs over the pirates who prowled the North Sea and the Channel. Once, in a tiny vessel crewed by only 17 men, he attacked and captured a Dunkirk privateer, undaunted by its complement of 120 sailors and 20 guns. Until the smoke cleared, the Dunkirk captain thought he had been bested by a full-size man-of-war.

De Ruyter had outlived two other wives by the time he married Anna, a sailor's widow with a background as modest and a Zeeland accent as thick as his own. Not long after the marriage, Michiel was persuaded to take the vice-admiral's position in Amsterdam because his country needed him. Reluctantly, the de Ruyters moved from Vlissingen to the republic's great city. Amsterdam, pleased to welcome such a distinguished national hero, granted him "great civic status," a distinction acknowledging him as a full freeman of the city and granting him equal rank with the city's governing class.

Visiting grandees, especially the heads of foreign navies, were fascinated by the earthy old sea dogs who commanded the Dutch fleet. Even the lowliest ranks referred to Michiel de Ruyter as *Bestevaer,* or "Granddad." One Spanish admiral marveled that de Ruyter dressed like the salt-stained captain of a cargo boat and lived in a modest house instead of a palace. A French aristocrat declared himself proud to be called a friend by this bluff, plain-speaking mariner.

The de Ruyters' lack of social pretensions did not stop them from taking a lively interest in the acquisition of wealth. Michiel had started buying stock at the age of 19 and added to his investment portfolio with the solid profits he made on his trading voyages.

As Michiel had risen through the ranks of the admiralty, he had received generous rewards for his naval successes and never failed to claim payment for any expenses incurred in the line of duty. When he captured ships, he took home a substantial share of the booty. He also had the right to purchase all the provisions required for his flagship and then sell them to the ship's cook at a considerable markup. Anna, endowed with a shrewd eye for a bargain, helped him find the cheapest sources of supply.

Though nowhere near as dangerous as her husband's, Anna's life had its own demands. Even after Michiel's success had transformed Anna into an admiral's lady, she never acquired any upper-class airs or graces. Like every good Dutch housewife, she made no distinction between cleanliness and godliness. Each day of the week—apart from the Sabbath, which was given over to the cleansing of the soul—brought its own set of prescribed tasks, in addition to those required daily. Anna, assisted by her daughter, her niece, and a pair of maidservants, scrupulously performed them all.

Two women put away clean linens in a large chest as a child wielding a kolf stick looks on. Foreigners often noted the pride Dutch householders took in maintaining a plentiful supply of immaculate linens. As one Englishman noted, Dutch beds were so high that climbing out of one in the middle of the night could result in a fatal injury, but "this comfort at least you will leave your friends, of having died in clean linen."

The obsession with domestic hygiene began outside the door. Donning their oldest aprons, and a pair of protective cuffs that covered their arms from wrist to elbow, Anna and other Dutch women set to work. Soon after daybreak, every Dutch town echoed with the sound of brooms and brushes. Every street was lined with scores of women, kneeling before their doorsteps as if in prayer, scrubbing their front steps and adjacent pavement until the stones acquired the dazzle of virgin snow and the bricks gleamed like rubies. "Every door," remarked an English visitor, whose own compatriots displayed a far more casual attitude toward dirt, "seems studded with diamonds."

Inside, once bedding was aired, pillows plumped, dishes washed, laundry finished, every stick of furniture dusted, all floors and walls and children scrutinized and treated against any signs of insect infestation, the women could turn to the weekly chores.

On Mondays those rooms reserved for the reception of visitors received a thorough dusting and polishing; on Tuesdays the bedrooms received the same treatment. Wednesdays called for the whole house to be gone over, top to bottom, from the basement passageway to the attic.

Thursdays brought the scrubbing and buffing of every object prone to stain or tarnish. Housemaids, however, considered Fridays the true bane of their existence, bringing yet another battle in the endless war against kitchen grease and the cellar's grime. But whatever the weekday, the maids might have to fetch and carry some 30 or 40 bucketfuls of water before their mistresses pronounced themselves satisfied.

"Dutchwomen pride themselves on the cleanliness of house and furniture to an unbelievable degree," reported one foreign visitor. "When they are obliged to allow a foreigner into the house they usually provide straw slippers in which they encase his feet, shoes and all."

Housework was not, however, the only job undertaken by Dutchwomen. Though they were excluded from political offices, women ran orphanages, old-age homes, hospitals, and houses of correction. They were active in commercial and business dealings, property management, family financial affairs, and the running of shops. As one observer noted, Dutchwomen "were generally bred to accounts, and affairs and labor as much as their husbands."

More unusual perhaps were the

Seventeenth-century domestic life unfolds in the rooms of this dollhouse, which includes a collector's cabinet *(middle right)* and a lying-in room for childbirth *(bottom center)*. Some 1,600 pieces of furniture, paintings, and fine objects were specially commissioned for the house by its wealthy owner.

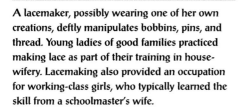

A lacemaker, possibly wearing one of her own creations, deftly manipulates bobbins, pins, and thread. Young ladies of good families practiced making lace as part of their training in house-wifery. Lacemaking also provided an occupation for working-class girls, who typically learned the skill from a schoolmaster's wife.

women who pursued careers as actors, writers, and artists. Despite the disapproval of men like Nicolaes Tulp, in 1655 Amsterdam opened its theater to its first actress, Ariane Noozeman, whose career flourished there. In the same decade, the writer Anna Maria van Schurman, who lived in Utrecht, published a Latin tract entitled *The Learned Maid, or Whether a Maid May Also Be a Scholar*. The answer, according to Schurman, was a resounding yes. To those who claimed scholarly pursuits were not appropriate for women, Schurman responded, "Whatsoever perfects and adorns the intellect of Man, that is fit and decent for a Christian woman."

Judith Leyster, born in Haarlem around 1609, enjoyed a successful career as a painter. Like Rembrandt, she did not come from an artistic family (her father was a weaver and brewery owner), and she may have first studied art as part of the family's weaving business, possibly to help with pattern design. Or perhaps she initially pursued an art career as a means of support after her father went bankrupt in 1624. Whatever her original motivations, her talent was undeniable. Leyster was in demand for portraits and for her many boisterous depictions of musicians, court jesters, drinkers, and others. A publication from the late 1620s described Leyster as an artist "who paints with a good, keen sense."

Anna de Ruyter led a much more traditional life than Noozeman, Schurman, and Leyster. After taking care of her house, she would ready herself to go out and do the marketing. She put on a freshly laundered apron, made sure her cap was properly in place, and—if the day was chilly—donned the long black hooded cloak called a *huik*. Anna's niece and daughter probably teased her about her fondness for this old-fashioned garment; hardly anybody wore the huik anymore except working-class women. Anna remained untroubled by these taunts. Back home in Zeeland the sailors' wives had always worn them, and if they were good enough for the quay side in Vlissingen, she thought, they were good enough for Amsterdam.

If she needed many provisions, Anna might bring a maid along to help carry them. Otherwise, she preferred to go out alone, shopping basket over her arm. Foreign friends were undoubtedly astonished to see an

admiral's wife doing her own household marketing. She may have been no less surprised when they told her that respectable matrons in their own countries would never have walked about the city in such a free and easy manner. The Dutch could be proud that much of the freedom enjoyed by the republic's women was a direct result of the relative safety of the streets, diligently patrolled by local officials.

Anna walked along the Warmoesstraat, the city's heart, passing some 200 shops crammed with the finest Bavarian porcelain, Italian majolica, bolts of silk from Lyon, and handsome Oriental tables inlaid with mother-of-pearl. Some of these items probably found their way into the de Ruyter home. Over the years, the de Ruyters' house had become well appointed as Michiel's career progressed, and the couple acquired more and more expensive furnishings, including a favorite easy chair covered in velvet.

As she approached the bustling market in Dam Square, Anna could hear the vendors' cries and smell their pungent wares: sweet raisins, rye bread, spices, herring. Here she purchased food for the family meals.

At the de Ruyters' home, dinner would begin and end with a prayer of thanks for Heaven's bounty. Afterward, if Michiel was ashore, he usually savored a glass of good French or Spanish wine, led the family in a session of psalm singing, or read aloud from the Bible while the women sewed. Some of their neighbors might spend evening hours playing card games, gambling with dice, or regaling guests with ditties from one of the latest printed song-books, but such pastimes seemed frivolous to the de Ruyters.

The admiral was a pious man, "a mirror of all Christian virtues," according to an old friend. He enjoyed nothing more than a good uplifting sermon, attending church not just on the Sabbath, but several times a week. He was a generous donor to worthy causes; after moving to Amsterdam, he continued sending money back home to Vlissingen, to relieve the sufferings of the poor.

Even when his naval duties kept him away for months on end, the admiral dominated the household. Anna, missing him, might have opened the handsome new atlas published by the mapmaker Joan Blaeu and turned its richly decorated pages to find the seas where Michiel was sailing. As she walked through the principal rooms of her house, she could contemplate the portraits of her husband and his fellow officers, the painted scenes of the ports he had visited and the battles he had fought. To ease the pain of separation, the couple kept up a constant flow of correspondence. Thanks to this habit, Anna was able to save her home, her family, and her husband's reputation from the wrath of a mob on that harrowing day in September 1672.

It was fortunate for everyone that she had. The Dutch navy

excelled under Michiel de Ruyter's leadership. They repeatedly defeated French and English fleets off the Dutch coast, and the war began to turn against the allies. Under William III's leadership, the army successfully fought back as well. In 1674 England withdrew from the fight. Within months, the French were forced out of the United Provinces, though the war raged on elsewhere.

Two years later, in 1676, Michiel de Ruyter was seriously wounded during a naval battle with the French and died within a week. His compatriots extolled him as one of his country's sav-

Traders, farmers, turbaned Eastern merchants, and black-garbed patricians make their way through the Dam, Amsterdam's bustling central square. Painted in 1656, the picture portrays the partially erected town hall, a baroque structure befitting the city's then burgeoning wealth. Only two decades later, however, the Dutch golden age would be in decline.

iors, a veritable "terror of the ocean" and "Hercules of the seas." His funeral drew admirers from every corner of the nation to watch his coffin be carried—in a five-hour-long procession—to the admiral's tomb. As the leading poets of the nation intoned their funeral orations, they had to compete with the thunder of a 24-gun salute from a frigate lying in the harbor.

But even in those days of deepest mourning, Anna de Ruyter continued to work and keep her household in order. While her husband's body lay in state before the burial, the prince of Orange sent Constantijn Huygens to pay a formal condolence call. But Anna was unable to receive the royal emissary. She had suffered a minor injury and taken to her bed. Huygens, inquiring further, was told that the widow had slipped and fallen while hanging laundry on the line.

Though peace with France was finally concluded in 1678, these past few years had marked a turning point for the Dutch. The glow of unrivaled prosperity had begun to dim. In 1689, William III, who had married Mary Stuart of England, daughter of King James, accepted joint rule of the island kingdom with his wife. William eventually favored England in the alliance. The United Provinces found their navy neglected and England surpassing them in trade. Their economy declined, and they lost their eminence. The Dutch no longer stood at the pinnacle of success.

But during the 17th century, the Dutch had created a legacy in art, science, business, and government that would long endure. Their age would be remembered as a golden one, when Amsterdam and the United Provinces had made their presence felt throughout the world.

Much Loved Dutch Children

Parents in the Netherlands lavished so much affection on their offspring that English-born Pilgrims, in Holland before sailing to America, complained that there was "too much kissing and cuddling going on." But when accused by foreigners or sterner Calvinists of spoiling their children, the Dutch often replied, "Cutting off the nose spoils the face."

These tender bonds began to form at birth, an occasion for often wild rejoicing. The day that a Dutch baby entered the world, relatives and neighbors gathered around to admire the new arrival and drink spiced wine. The father, wearing a feathered satin cap, hung a lace-trimmed ornament on the door to announce his new son or daughter. The entire community then welcomed the baby by temporarily exempting the family from certain duties and taxes.

Most Dutchwomen, even the most prosperous, breast-fed their infants rather than farming them out to wet nurses, as some women did in France and Italy. Furnishings in a household with children usually included a woven-straw nursing chair known as a *bakermat* on which the mother reclined while breast-feeding. If she grew ill or died, a wet nurse would be employed, but only in the home, never out.

Parents took great care to nurture their children, and the Dr. Spock of 17th-century Holland, Stephanus Blankaart, had plenty of sage advice to offer them. Parents, he urged, should provide a nutritious diet for their children, including fresh fruits and vegetables. Potty training should not begin too early, and when the time was ripe, parents should offer the child a toy so that using the *kakstoel,* or potty, was a fun event. As for discipline, parents would do best to spare the rod, instead employing "sweet admonition to lead [children's] thoughts to better ways."

The picture of health in a portrait by Frans Hals, this child looks utterly content even with her stiff lace cap and collar. Under their layers of burdensome clothing, young Dutch children also wore whale-bone corsets to prevent bone deformation.

A mother, her foot propped on a portable warmer heated with burning peat, lovingly breast-feeds her baby while her older child offers a bowl to the pet dog. This scene of domestic tranquillity, painted by Pieter de Hooch and reminiscent of the Madonna and child, represented a Dutch ideal.

Delighted children clamor around
a man playing a *rommel pot,* made
from a pig's bladder stretched over
an earthenware jar partly filled with
water. Sliding a reed up and down
through a hole in the bladder created
a sound like a squealing pig.

The Republic of Children

Standing on a just scrubbed floor, a mischievous-looking child clutches a *kolf* stick while a playmate waits outside. The game of kolf, popular with children and adults alike, was a forerunner of golf.

From dawn until dusk, the streets of Dutch towns swarmed with little people of all social classes, creating what amounted to an exuberant, unruly republic of children. Houses were generally small, and to keep them tidy, mothers shooed their younger children outdoors. There they played in all but the most inclement weather with an abundant variety of toys: kites, hoops, jump ropes, hobbyhorses, drums, miniature windmills, stilts, marbles, and bugles. As soon as school let out, the older children joined in. Games of every kind exercised their imaginations, including blindman's bluff, leapfrog, I spy, and knucklebones.

When the novelty of all this play wore off, some children would torment stray dogs and cats—and adults as well. Many an unfortunate passerby was jeered or pelted with rocks. Foreign visitors, ready targets of abuse in their strange garb, wrote of the children's disrespect and lack of discipline. Local church councils complained about children kicking balls outside during Sunday services. But such objections brought little relief; doting Dutch parents agreed with this advice from a contemporary moralist: "Children should not be kept on too tight a rein, but allowed to exercise their childishness. . . . Otherwise they will be against learning before they know what learning is."

In this detail from a family portrait, two sisters nibble on fruit while their roguish brother gleefully holds up a cat that has just scratched the sister at right.

153

Gardens of Learning

Despite the punishment he is about to administer, a weary schoolmaster appears to have no control over his little ladies and lords of misrule. Classrooms packed with pupils emitted a notorious din; the Dutch had a saying that it was easier to pass a blacksmith's shop than a school.

Schools, proclaimed the Deputized Councils of Holland in 1623, "are like gardens, where the love of God and respect for legal authority must be transplanted into the young." So for all Dutch children but the very wealthy, who had private tutors, and the very poor, who couldn't afford the fees, at least a few years of childhood were taken up with getting an education.

Between the ages of three and seven, children attended an "infant school," where they learned their ABCs and the Lord's Prayer and girls began to learn the arts of dressmaking and knitting. This rudimentary education was often delivered in conditions of barely contained chaos: smoky rooms with children sprawled about the floor and the teacher's bed in the corner.

Many seven-year-olds went on to "junior school." The curriculum consisted of sacred history, reading, writing, and—critical in such a commercial economy—arithmetic. But girls often dropped out before they learned to write, and many boys left to pursue an apprenticeship. Those who kept on endured five years of learning by rote. For 330 days of each year, pupils filed up to a master's desk to deliver their recitations, and woe to the unfortunate student who incurred his wrath: Punishment with whip or cane was common, if not always effective.

Teachers were grossly underpaid and often unqualified. "Those who could barely write their names rushed at once to schoolteaching," complained one master. But they made basic education fairly accessible in Holland, resulting in a literacy rate that was among the highest in Europe.

An artist teaches his son the finer points of drawing while his wife sharpens another pen for them to use. Boys as young as eight could be apprenticed to a master, sometimes to their own father.

Celebrating Children's Holidays

In spite of Calvinist restrictions on the public celebration of Catholic holy days, many Dutch families continued to observe two such days that held special appeal for children: Pentecost and the Feast of Saint Nicholas. Pentecost blended the religious feast marking the arrival of the Holy Spirit with the pagan tradition of May Day, which welcomed spring. A procession of children led by a *pinksterbruid,* or Pentecost bride, would wind through the village streets singing merrily. The pinksterbruid wore a white robe and carried a cup into which bystanders plunked coins. The festivities also included dancing around a Maypole festooned with flowers.

Saint Nicholas's day was celebrated inside the home. On December 5, children left shoes by the hearth and sang songs to the saint, who was expected to slide down their chimney. The next morning the household tingled with excitement. Sometimes candy skittered across the floor from an unknown source, fooling younger children into thinking it had come from the fireplace. Good children pulled treats and gifts from their shoes, perhaps a gingerbread saint or a John the Baptist doll. Naughty ones were less fortunate—they received a switch for spankings.

A little girl jealously guards her new doll and pail of treats while her brother, holding a new kolf stick, laughs at an older, crying brother who has received a birch switch. Though his parents may have thought he deserved the switch, a woman in the background, perhaps his grand-mother, beckons the disconsolate boy to a curtained bed, where she may give him a present anyway.

Wearing a paper crown and a white apron over his trousers, a young boy dressed as the pinksterbruid, trailed by a girl acting as his train bearer, accepts a donation from a man as the very short procession passes by *(left).* Another spectator, a smiling baby, waves a *pinksterbloem,* or Pentecost flower.

GLOSSARY

Almshouse: a home for the poor funded by private donations.

Annate: originally, a tax paid to the papal curia by a clergyman appointed to a minor position that carried with it a guaranteed fixed yearly income; by the 15th century, included the entire first year's income, or "first fruits," from higher-level benefices, such as a bishopric or heads of monasteries.

Augsburg Confession: the Lutheran confession of faith, presented June 25, 1530, to Emperor Charles V at the Diet of Augsburg, which set forth in its first 21 articles the essential Lutheran doctrines, still used today by the Lutheran Church, and detailed in its final seven articles systemic abuses alleged to have become part of Catholicism.

Bakermat: in the Netherlands, a woven-straw nursing chair used by a mother or wet nurse when breast-feeding an infant.

Barbary pirate: any of a group of sailor-outlaws from the Barbary Coast states of Algeria, Tunisia, Tripoli, and Morocco who terrorized ships in the Mediterranean from the 16th to the 19th century, pillaging cargoes, and either holding crews and passengers for ransom or selling them into slavery.

Baroque: a style of art and architecture that began in Italy in the latter half of the 16th century and spread through much of Europe, characterized by its grandeur, richness, drama, vitality, and complexity of design.

Beeldenstorm: in 1566, the rioting and desecration of Roman Catholic churches and convents by the lower classes throughout the 17 provinces of the Netherlands in response to the church's economic and political practices as well as to its religious teachings.

Beggars: name given to the approximately 200 Protestant and Catholic members of the lesser nobility who in 1566 presented a petition to the regent of the Netherlands, Margaret of Parma, requesting a convocation of the States-General, suspension of the heresy edicts and the Inquisition, and institution of religious tolerance.

Bourse: in some continental European countries, the stock exchange at which stocks and bonds are traded and, at which, in earlier times, other kinds of financial and trading transactions took place.

Buizen: the Dutch name for a long herring ship with three masts, two of which could be lowered to reduce wind resistance and rolling, permitting easier tending of the nets and processing of the fish on board.

Bundschuh: a shoe worn by peasants, first used as a symbol of peasant rebellion in the mid-15th century and again in the great peasant uprising of 1524-1525.

Burgher: in German and Dutch towns and cities, a member of the middle class, particularly one who was well-to-do.

Burgomasters: in Germany and the Netherlands, the mayor or chief magistrate of a town or city whose duties and power varied but who was generally responsible for the administration of the municipality.

Bursa: a residential hall at a medieval university.

Chiaroscuro: the technique of representing light and shade in a pictorial work of art.

Cooper: one who makes or repairs wooden casks, barrels, or tubs.

Count: a European nobleman who ranks below a marquis.

Crossbow: a weapon, more powerful than a bow and arrow but of similar appearance, with grooves on the wooden or metal stock to direct an arrow or other projectile at a target.

Diet of Worms: the assembly of the German estates of the Holy Roman Empire held in April 1521 at Worms, Germany, at which Martin Luther refused to recant his teachings and was banned in the empire by the Edict of Worms.

Dike: a man-made embankment created to form a barrier between a natural or man-made waterway and dry land.

Doublet: a man's close-fitting, padded and waisted jacket, worn over a shirt and popular in Europe from the 15th to the 17th century, with the style and cut varying over the years.

Duchy: the territory of a duke or duchess.

Duke: a nobleman of the highest hereditary rank after that of a prince; a sovereign male ruler of an independent European duchy.

Edict of Worms: the imperial decree that proclaimed Martin Luther to be a heretic and outlaw within the Holy Roman Empire, authorized his arrest or execution, prohibited him from preaching, and barred the copying, printing, sale, or possession of his writings.

Elector: from about 1356 until 1806, any of the seven, later 10, princes and archbishops entitled to participate in the election of the Holy Roman emperor.

Engraving: the act or art of cutting or etching a design into a hard surface, such as wood or metal; a print made from such a surface.

Etching: the act or art of producing a design on a hard surface, such as metal, through the corrosive action of acid; a print made from such a surface.

Evangelical: the name by which the reform movement in Germany and Switzerland was called prior to 1529, after which the word Protestant was used; any Christian church believing that salvation is received directly through faith in Christ and not acquired through sacraments and good works.

Excommunication: an ecclesiastical censure in which a person, city, or state is deprived of the rights of church membership, including the right to participate in all sacraments except baptism and last rites.

Fiat: an arbitrary order, sanction, or decree made by an absolute ruler having the ability and authority to enforce it.

Florin: in the Middle Ages, a gold coin, first minted in Florence, Italy, in 1252; any of several gold coins similar to the Florentine coin.

Fluit: a Dutch-invented cargo ship, inexpensive to build and operate and usually unarmed, with a broad-bottomed hull designed to carry cargo ranging from 200 to 500 tons and capable of sailing with about a third the number of crewmen as English cargo ships.

Frauenhaus: a brothel; a house of prostitution.

Frigate: a fast-moving, medium-sized, three-masted fighting ship of the 17th, 18th, and 19th centuries, carrying between 24 and 56 guns, primarily on its one gun deck; used mainly as naval scouts, as escorts for merchant convoys, and as privateers.

Genre: a category of music, art, or literature marked by a distinctive style, form, technique, or content.

Gorget: a collar worn with upper body armor to protect the wearer's throat.

Gothic: a style of architecture, painting, sculpture, and music prevalent in northern Europe from the 12th through the 15th centuries, with architecture, the style's most important medium, characterized by pointed arches, flying buttresses, and rib vaulting.

Grace: the freely given and unmerited divine love, protection, and favor of God, viewed by the Catholic Church as being channeled to humans through church sacraments but by Protestants as being dependent upon the faith of the believer.

Grandee: a Spanish or Portuguese nobleman of the highest rank.

Guilder: formerly, any of the various gold coins used by the German states and the Netherlands; today, the basic monetary unit of the Netherlands.

Guilds: associations of craftsmen, artisans, or merchants that organized, regulated, and restricted trade in products, crafts, or services, and that were active in the political and civic affairs of most medieval and Renaissance cities.

Hedge preaching: religious services held in fields in the countryside.

Heresy: prior to the Reformation, any opinion, especially one expressed by a baptized believer, that was in opposition to Roman Catholic dogma.

Holy Roman Empire: a loosely federated, primarily Germanic, central-European political entity that existed from the coronation of Otto I in 962 until 1806 and included a patchwork of political relationships, such as duchies, counties, cities, and principalities.

Huik: a long black hooded cloak of ancient origin.

Humanists: scholars, both secular and religious, who emphasized the study of ancient biblical and classical sources and who were instrumental in the Renaissance revival of interest in Greek and Roman writings, values, and philosophy.

Hutsepot: a Dutch stew containing mutton or beef, green vegetables, parsnips, prunes, vinegar, and lemon juice, boiled with fat and ginger.

Imperial Diet: from the 12th century to 1805, the general assembly of the Holy Roman Empire, held annually in different cities throughout the empire.

Indulgence: in Roman Catholicism, the remission by the church of time to be spent in purgatory as punishment for sins for which the penitent has not yet done the penance imposed on him by the priest in confession.

Infidel: one who opposes or does not believe in a particular religion, especially Christianity or Islam.

Inquisition: an ecclesiastical tribunal established by the Roman Catholic Church in 1231 to pursue and punish those committing heresy and witchcraft, later extended to include those committing blasphemy and sacrilege as well.

Junker: a wealthy domineering nobleman, particularly of

northeastern Germany; also, spoiled noble youth.

Kakstoel: in the Netherlands, a child's potty.

Kermis: in the low countries, a local, annual outdoor fair or festival usually held on the feast day of the local patron saint or on the anniversary of the local church's dedication.

Knucklebones: a game played by children worldwide since antiquity, with variations in the rules and materials used, but generally consisting of five stones, bones, or seeds that are tossed into the air, the object being to catch as many as possible before they fall to earth.

Kolf: a popular game, similar to golf, played in the Netherlands.

Landgrave: in medieval German states from 1130 through the 20th century, a provincial count with jurisdiction over a large territory, responsible only to the king, with power and rank equal to that of a duke.

Landsknechte: German mercenary soldiers.

Letters of marque: documents issued by a political entity, such as a nation or autonomous principality, authorizing a private citizen to seize the property or citizens of another nation, or to equip and operate a ship to prey on the enemy's ships for this purpose.

Lord: a man of high rank in feudal society, especially a king, nobleman, or wealthy landowner; a landowner who granted livestock (and possibly land) to a farmer in return for stipulated goods and services, including labor and military service.

Low Countries: the region of northwest Europe that today consists of Belgium, the Netherlands, Luxembourg, and parts of northern France.

Magistrate: a civil official empowered to administer and enforce the law; a local judicial officer with limited jurisdiction but generally having the authority to investigate and try minor cases.

Majolica: a type of tin-glazed pottery with a white, opaque surface on which a design is painted, used since ancient times, but popularized in 15th-century Italy; similar earthenware from France, Spain, Germany, and Scandinavia is known as faience and in the Netherlands as delft.

Marzipan: a confection made from ground almonds or almond paste, egg whites, and sugar, used to fill candies and pastries or molded into decorative shapes.

Miller: a person who owns, works in, and/or operates a mill, especially a mill that grinds grain into flour.

Ming dynasty: Chinese dynasty (1368-1644) noted for its achievements in education, foreign trade, and the arts, especially porcelain, textiles, and painting.

Musico: a drinking hall with a small orchestra.

Naturalia: natural items, such as skeletons, preserved human organs, and other anatomical, botanical, or mineral items.

Netherlands, the: at the time of the Reformation, 17 provinces, comprising modern-day Holland, Belgium, Luxembourg, and part of France.

Ordination: the act or ceremony investing a person with ministerial or priestly authority and functions.

Papal bull: a letter or official document from the pope, sealed with a round leaden seal called a bulla.

Papal nuncio: a papal representative of the highest rank,

permanently accredited to a civil government.

Penance: in the Roman Catholic Church, a sacrament that consists of contrition, confession to a priest, acceptance of punishment, and absolution; one of the sacraments retained by Luther, but in an Evangelical form, with the sinner permitted to appeal to Christian laity as well as to the clergy for forgiveness based on his or her faith in God's grace.

Penitential fees: annual fees collected by the Roman Catholic Church from priests who had taken mates and fathered children, used both as a penalty and as an expression of remorse for the sin without necessarily ending the state of concubinage.

Pike: a weapon of war consisting of a long wooden shaft with a pointed steel head, used by foot soldiers.

Pillory: a wooden device consisting of a framework with holes for the head and hands, in which offenders were locked for public ridicule.

Polder: a low-lying tract of land reclaimed from a body of water and protected by dikes.

Predestination: the doctrine that all things, including the salvation or damnation of individual souls, are preordained by God.

Prelate: a high-ranking member of the clergy, especially a bishop.

Privateer: an armed, privately owned ship authorized by a government during wartime to prey upon and capture or sink the warships or merchant ships of the enemy or, during peace time, those of pirates.

Procurator: an agent, attorney, or officer authorized to manage the affairs of another.

Protectorate: in international law, the relationship between an autonomous political entity that surrenders part of its sovereignty to a superior power in return for protection.

Purgatory: in the Roman Catholic Church, an intermediate place or state of punishment where souls of those who have died in a state of grace are punished for and purged of their unrepented or unpunished minor sins before being admitted into heaven.

Pyre: a pile of wood or other combustible material for a bonfire.

Rack: an instrument of torture consisting of a large frame with rollers at either end to which the limbs were fastened and upon which the body was stretched.

Regent: one who rules during the minority, absence, or incapacitation of a monarch; in Amsterdam, the collective name given to the 36 governing burghers on the city council.

Roman Curia: in the Roman Catholic Church, the name given the papal bureaucracy in Rome that assists the pope; also called the papal curia.

Rommel pot: a noisemaking device made from a pig's bladder stretched over an earthenware jar partly filled with water. By sliding a reed up and down through a hole in the bladder, the player created a sound like a squealing pig.

Schism: a serious division or difference of opinion among two or more factions within a group; a formal division within a religious body over doctrinal differences.

Schmalkaldic League: a defensive alliance entered into in 1531 by the Protestant princes and more than a dozen of the imperial cities in the Holy Roman Empire to defend Lutheran churches from attacks by the Catholic emperor. The league was destroyed by the emperor's forces in 1547.

Sea Beggars: a small fleet of 30 ships organized in 1568 by Louis of Nassau, with a fiercely anti-Catholic crew of noblemen, merchants, fishermen, and ruffians; the fleet plied the English Channel preying upon Spanish ships and plundering the Dutch coast under letters of marque from William of Orange.

Sea dog: a very experienced sailor.

Seignory: under the manorial system, the domain of a lord (seigneur), which might be a large territory or only a small rural estate hierarchically organized for self-sufficiency.

Silverpoint: a drawing technique using a silver-tipped penlike instrument and specially prepared paper or parchment.

Solicitor: the chief legal officer of a city, town, county, or government department.

Stadholder: in the Netherlands from the 15th through the 18th century, the provincial executive officer or chief magistrate for a province.

Stuyver (Stiver): a coin made of nickel, once used in the Netherlands and worth five Dutch cents.

Tally plank: a board on which innkeepers kept track of how many drinks each customer had ordered.

Tanner: one who converts animal hides into leather.

Tenth Penny: in the Netherlands, a 10 percent tax exacted on every commercial transaction, imposed by the duke of Alva to finance his army of occupation in the country.

Thaler: any of various silver coins used as currency in many of the German states from 1519 to 1873.

Usury: excessively high interest charged to a borrower for a loan.

Vatican: the ecclesiastical seat of the Roman Catholic Church and the official residence of the Pope.

Vellum: a thin, supple material made of calfskin, lambskin, or kidskin used for writing, drawing, and for the pages and bindings of books.

Virginal: a small keyboard instrument similar to a harpsichord but rectangular in shape, with no legs.

Wanderjahre: literally, "wander years." A period of several years when young craftsmen visited reputable workshops throughout their general region to train with masters of their craft.

Weaver: one who produces fabric from thread by interlacing two sets of yarns on a loom so that the threads cross each other at right angles.

Weigh house: the building in Amsterdam where peasants' produce was weighed for tax purposes and where, on the upper floors, guilds were housed.

Weir: a dam across a stream, river, or canal used to raise the water level or divert its flow; a wattle fence in a stream or small river used for catching fish.

Woodcut: a pictorial engraving carved on a block of wood used in printing, also called a woodblock.

PRONUNCIATION GUIDE

Adriaan Adriaanszoon (AH-dree-yahn AH-dree-yahns-zohn)
Albrecht Dürer (AHL-brehkt DEW-rehr)
Allstedt (AHL-shteht)
Andreas Karlstadt (ahn-DRAY-ahs KAHRL-shtaht)
Anna Maria van Schurman (AH-nah mah-REE-ah vahn SHKHEWR-mahn)
Anthony van Dyck (AHN-toh-nee vahn dyke)
Augsburg (OWGS-boorg)
Bakermat (BAH-kuhr-maht)
Basel (BAH-zuhl)
Batavia (bah-TAH-vee-yah)
Beeldenstorm (BAYL-duhn-stohrm)
Bestevaer (BEHS-tuh-vahr)
Brabant (BRAH-bahnt)
Breestraat (BRAY-straht)
Buizen (BOY-zuhn)
Bundschuh (BOOND-shoo)
Capelle (kah-PEHL-luh)
Casimir (KHAH-zee-meer)
Caspar Barlaeus (kahs-PAHR bahr-LAY-uhs)
Claes Pieterszoon (klahs PEE-tuhrs-zohn)
Constantijn Huygens (KOHN-stahn-tine HOY-guhns)
Cornelis Tromp (kohr-NAY-lihs trohmp)
Desiderius Erasmus (day-zee-DAY-ree-yuhs ay-RAHS-muhs)
Donauworth (DOH-now-vuhrth)
Elbe (EHL-buh)
Enkhuizen (EHNK-hoy-zuhn)
Erfurt (EHR-foort)
Fluit (floyt)
Frankenhausen (FRAHN-kuhn-how-zuhn)
Frankfurt (FRAHNK-foort)
Frans Banning Cocq (frahns BAHN-ihng kohk)
Frans Hals (frahns hahls)
Franz von Sickingen (frahnts fahn ZIHK-ihng-uhn)
Frauenhaus (FROW-uhn-hows)
Frederick Ruysch (FRAY-duh-rihk royshkh)
Fugger (FOO-guhr)
Gabriel Zwilling (GAH-bree-yehl TSVIHL-ihng)
Geertge Dircx (GAYRT-hkhuh dihrx)
Gelderland (HKHEHL-duhr-lahnd)
Georg Spalatin (GAY-ahrg shpah-LAH-tihn)
Gijsbrecht van Aemstel (HKHEYES-brehkht vahn AHM-stuhl)
Gouda (HKHOW-dah)
Groote Visscherij (GROH-tuh VIHS-khkuh-reye)
Guillaume Farel (gee-YOHM FAH-rehl)

Hans Holbein (hahns HOHL-bine)
Hans Tausen (hahns TOW-zuhn)
Heinrich von Kettenbach (HINE-reehkh fahn KEHT-ehn-bahkh)
Hendrickje Stoffels (HEHN-drihk-yuh STOHF-uhls)
Hendrik Uylenburgh (HEHN-drihk OY-luhn-buhrgh)
Hesse (hehs-uh)
Hieronymous Bosch (heer-OH-nee-muhs bohshkh)
Hoorn (hohrn)
Huik (hoyk)
Hutsepot (HUHT-suh-poht)
IJ (eye)
IJssel (EYE-suhl)
Ingolstadt (IHN-gohl-shtaht)
Jan Hus (yahn hoos)
Jan Lievens (yahn LEE-vuhns)
Jan Six (yahn sihx)
Jan Vermeer (yahn vehr-MAYR)
Java (YAH-vah)
Joannes Tenbogaert (YOH-ahn-nuhs tehn-BOH-hkhahrt)
Johannes Blaeu (yoh-HAHN-uhs blow)
Joost van den Vondel (yohst vahn duhn VOHN-duhl)
Jorg (yuhrkh)
Judith Leyster (YEW-diht LEYE-stuhr)
Kakstoel (KAHK-stool)
Katherine von Bora (kah-tuhr-EEN-uh fahn BOH-rah)
Keizersgracht (KEYE-zuhrs-hkhrahkht)
Kitzingen (KIHTS-ihn-guhn)
Konrad Celtis (KOHN-rahd KEHL-tihs)
Konstanz (kahn-SHTAHNTS)
Landsknechte (LAHNTS-knehkh-tuh)
Leiden (LEYE-duhn)
Leipzig (LEYE-ptsig)
Leonhard Koppe (LAY-ohn-hahrt KAHP-uh)
Leonhard Stochel (LAY-ohn-hahrt SHTUH-hkhuhl)
Lucas Cranach (LOO-kahs KRAHN-ahkh)
Lucas Friedrich (LOO-kahs FREE-drihkh)
Ludwig von Helfenstein (LOOT-vihg fahn HEHL-fuhn-shtine)
Mainz (meye-uhnts)
Mansfeld (MAHNS-fehld)
Marburg (MAHR-boorg)
Martin Schongauer (MAHR-tihn SHOHN-gow-uhr)
Matthaus Schwarz (mah-TAY-uhs shvahrts)
Mechelen (MEHKH-uhl-uhn)
Memmingen (MEHM-ihng-uhn)
Michael Wolgemut (MEE-kah-ehl VOHL-guh-moot)

Michiel de Ruyter (mee-HKHEEL duh ROY-tuhr)
Mosel (MOH-zuhl)
Mühlhausen (MEWL-how-zuhn)
Münster (MEWN-stuhr)
Niederweisel (NEE-duhr-veye-zuhl)
Nürnberg (NEWRN-behrg)
Odenwald (OH-dehn-vahld)
Olav Pedersson (OH-lahf PAY-duhr-sohn)
Philipp Melanchthon (FIHL-ihp may-LAHNKH-tohn)
Pieter de Hooch (PEE-tuhr duh hohkh)
Pieter Lastman (PEE-tuhr LAHST-mahn)
Pinksterbloem (PIHNK-stuhr-bloom)
Pinksterbruid (PIHNK-stuhr-broyt)
Rembrandt van Rijn (REHM-brahnt vahn rine)
Rommel pot (ROHM-muhl poht)
Sastrow (ZAHS-trohf)
Schmalkald (SHMAHL-kahld)
Schooneveld (SHKHOH-nuh-vehld)
Sigmund von Lupfen (ZEEKH-moont fahn LOOP-fuhn)
Simeon Engelhardt (ZEE-mee-yohn EHN-guhl-hahrt)
Sinter Klaas (SIHN-tuhr klahs)
Speyer (SHPEYE-uhr)
Stephan Carl Behaim (SHTAY-fahn kahrl BAY-hime)
Stephanus Blankaert (STAY-fah-nuhs BLAHN-kahrt)
Stralsund (SHTRAHL-zoond)
Stühlingen (SHTEW-lihng-uhn)
Texel (TEHKS-uhl)
Thomas Müntzer (TOH-mahs MEWN-tsuhr)
Torgau (TOHR-gow)
Trier (TREE-ehr)
Ulrich von Hutten (OOL-rihkh fahn HOOT-uhn)
Utrecht (EW-trehkht)
Van der Werff (vahn dehr vehrf)
Vlissingen (VLIHS-sihn-hkhuhn)
Wanderjahre (VAHN-duhr-yah-ruh)
Warmoesstraat (VAHR-moos-straht)
Wartburg (VAHRT-boorg)
Waterland (VAH-tuhr-lahnd)
Weinsberg (VINES-behrg)
Weisenau (VEYE-zuh-now)
Willibald Pirkheimer (VIHL-lee-bahld PIHRK-heye-muhr)
Wisselbank (VIHS-suhl-bahnk)
Wittenberg (VIHT-uhn-behrg)
Worms (vohrms)
Württemberg (VEWR-tehm-behrg)
Zeeland (ZAY-lahnd)
Zuider Zee (ZOY-dehr zay)

ACKNOWLEDGMENTS AND PICTURE CREDITS

ACKNOWLEDGMENTS

The editors wish to thank the following individuals and institutions for their valuable assistance in the preparation of this volume:

Florence Aalbers, Rijksmuseum, Amsterdam; Renata Antoniou, Graphische Sammlung Albertina, Vienna; Stéphane Hautekeete, Conservateur, Cabinet des Dessins, Muséees Royaux des Beaux-Arts de Belgique, Bruxelles; Mary Ison and staff, Library of Congress, Washington, D.C.; Ilse Jung, Kunsthistorisches Museum, Vienna; Benjamin Kaplan, University of Iowa, Iowa City; Heidrun Klein, Bildarchiv Preussischer Kulturbesitz, Berlin; Bernd Schaefer, Schlossmuseum, Gotha, Germany; Jutta Strehle, Stiftung Luthergedenkstätten in Sachsen-Anhalt, Wittenberg, Germany, and Reading Room staff of the Folger Shakespeare Library, Washington, D.C.

PICTURE CREDITS

The sources for the illustrations that appear in this volume are listed below. Credits from left to right are separated by semicolons; from top to bottom by dashes.

Cover: Rijksmuseum, Amsterdam (detail). **1-5:** Artothek/Joachim Blauel, Peissenberg, Alte Pinakothek, Munich, details from *A Tax Collector with his Wife* by Marius van Reymerswaele. **6, 7:** Gavin Hellier/Tony Stone Images. **8-11:** Art by John Drummond, © Time Life Inc., based on a photo from Schapowalow/Dieter, Hamburg. **12, 13:** Map by John Drummond, © Time Life Inc. **14, 15:** Christoph Sandig/Artothek, Peissenberg/Museum der bild. Künste, Leipzig, *Martin Luther as Junker Jörg* (detail) by Lucas Cranach the Elder. **16, 17:** Stiftung Luthergedenkstätten in Sachsen-Anhalt, Wittenberg; Archiv für Kunst und Geschichte (AKG), Berlin. **18:** Erich Lessing/Art Resource, N.Y. **19:** Schlossmuseum Gotha, Germany, Kupferstichkabinett. **20, 21:** Stiftung Luthergedenkstätten in Sachsen-Anhalt, photo © Wilfried Kirsch, Wittenberg. **23:** *Erasmus of Rotterdam* by Hans Holbein the Younger from a private collection on loan to The National Gallery, London. **24:** Sächsische Landesbibliothek-Staats-und Universitätsbibliothek Dresden, Dezernat Deutsche Fotothek/Rabich. **25:** Herzog Anton Ulrich-Museum, Braunschweig, museum photo by B. P. Keiser. **26, 27:** Mary Evans Picture Library, London. **28, 29:** AKG, Berlin; Stiftung Luthergedenkstätten in Sachsen-Anhalt, photo © Wilfried Kirsch, Wittenberg. **30:** AKG, Berlin. **33:** Fotomas Index, West Wickham, Kent. **34:** Jürgen Maria Pietsch, Spröda, courtesy of Stadtkirche, Wittenberg. **35:** Stiftung Luthergedenkstätten in Sachsen-Anhalt, photo © Wilfried Kirsch, Wittenberg. **37:** AKG, Berlin/Stadtbibliothek, Dessau—Stiftung Luthergedenkstätten in Sachsen-Anhalt, photo © Wilfried Kirsch, Wittenberg. **38:** Schlossmuseum Gotha, Germany, photo by Lutz Ebhardt, Wechmar—Stiftung Luthergedenkstätten in Sachsen-Anhalt, photo © Wilfried Kirsch, Wittenberg (2). **39:** Bildarchiv Claus Hansmann, Munich. **40, 41:** Jürgen Maria Pietsch, Spröda, courtesy of Stadtkirche, Wittenberg (details). **43:** Waltraud Klammet, Ohlstadt, Germany. **44:** AKG, Berlin/Museum Würzburg. **47:** Bildarchiv Claus Hansmann, Munich. **49:** Staatliche Museen zu Berlin-Preussischer Kulturbesitz, Kupferstichkabinett, photo by Jörg P. Anders. Quotation taken from *When Fathers Ruled* by Steve Ozment, Copyright © 1983 by the President and Fellows of Harvard College. Reprinted by permission of Harvard University Press. **50, 51:** Bildarchiv Preussischer Kulturbesitz, Berlin; Stiftung Luthergedenkstätten in Sachsen-Anhalt, photo © Wilfried Kirsch, Wittenberg. **52:** Scala/Art Resource, N.Y. **53:** Erich Lessing, Culture and Fine Arts Archive, Vienna/ Graphische Sammlung Albertina, Vienna. **54:** Staatliche Museen zu Berlin-Preussischer Kulturbesitz, Kupferstichkabinett, photo Jörg P. Anders. **55:** Graphische Sammlung Albertina, Vienna. **56:** Erich Lessing/Art Resource, N.Y. **57:** AKG, Berlin/Erich Lessing. **58:** Scala/Art Resource, N.Y. **59:** Copyright The British Museum, London. **60, 61:** Artothek/Blauel/Gnamm, Peissenberg, Alte Pinakothek, Munich. **62, 63:** Gianni Dagli Orti, Paris. **64, 65:** AKG, Paris/Kunsthistorisches Museum, Vienna. **67:** Artephot/Schneiders. **68:** AKG, Berlin/Staatsarchiv, Münster, Germany. **70, 71:** Bildarchiv Preussischer Kulturbesitz, Berlin—Herzog Anton Ulrich-Museum, Braunschweig, photo Bernd-Peter Keiser. **72, 73:** Bildarchiv Foto Marburg, Germany. **75:** AKG, Berlin/Bibl. Publique et Universitaire, Genève/Erich Lessing; Gianni Dagli Orti, Paris. **76, 77:** Graphische Sammlung Albertina, Vienna. **78:** Bildarchiv Foto Marburg—Photo Hubert Josse/Musée du Prado, Madrid. **80, 81:** Erich Lessing, Culture and Fine Arts Archive, Vienna/Kunsthistorisches Museum, Gemäldegalerie, Vienna; Erich Lessing, Culture and Fine Arts Archive, Vienna/Narodni Galerie, Prague (2). **82, 83:** Erich Lessing, Culture and Fine Arts Archive, Vienna/Kunsthistorisches Museum, Gemäldegalerie, Vienna. **85:** Agencja Fotograficzna, *Orleta*, fot. Maciej Bronarski, Print Room of the Warsaw University Library, Poland, Zb. Krol. Wol. 755, pl.8. **86:** Staatliche Museen zu Berlin-Preussischer Kulturbesitz, Gemäldegalerie, photo Jörg P. Anders. **87:** Rijksmuseum, Amsterdam. **88, 89:** Gianni Dagli Orti, Paris. **91:** Rijksmuseum, Amsterdam (detail). **92, 93:** Copyright Bibliothèque royale Albert Ier, Cabinet des Estampes, Bruxelles, *Ship and Soldiers Attack Walled City of Briel* by F. Hogenberg, M 413/123 S.N° folio. **94, 95:** Rijksmuseum, Amsterdam. **97:** Copyright Bibliothèque royale Albert Ier, Bruxelles. **98, 99:** Amsterdams Historisch Museum, *The Return to Amsterdam of the Second Expedition to the East Indies* (detail) by Hendrick Vroom; Coll. Nederlands Scheepvaartmuseum, Amsterdam (detail). **100, 101:** Christie's Images, London/Bridgeman Art Library, London; Zuiderzeemuseum (detail); Christie's Images, London/Bridgeman Art Library, London. **102, 103:** Ferens Art Gallery, Hull City Museums and Art Galleries/Bridgeman Art Library, London; Coll. Nederlands Scheepvaartmuseum, Amsterdam (detail); Rijksmuseum, Amsterdam (detail). **104, 105:** Rijksmuseum, Amsterdam (detail); Atlas Van Stolk, Rotterdam (detail). **106:** Gerbrand van den Eeckhout, *Four Officers of the Amsterdam Coopers' and Wine-Rackers' Guild*, © National Gallery, London. **107:** Museum Boijmans Van Beuningen, Rotterdam (detail). **108, 109:** Instituut Collectie Nederland. **111:** Johnny van Haeften Gallery, London/Bridgeman Art Library, London. **112:** Artothek, Peissenberg/Gemäldegalerie, Dresden (detail). **114, 115:** Frans Halsmuseum, Haarlem; © Staatsgalerie Stuttgart, *Kunstliebhaber im Atelier eines Malers* (detail) by Pieter Codde. **117:** Walters Art Gallery, Baltimore. **118, 119:** Wadsworth Atheneum, Hartford. Gift of J. Pierpont Morgan; Wadsworth Atheneum, Hartford. J. Pierpont Morgan Collection; courtesy of the Arthur M. Sackler Gallery, Smithsonian Institution, Washington, D.C. (accession # S1987.391)—Byzantine Collection, Dumbarton Oaks, Washington, D.C.—guitar by Joachim Tielke, National Museum of American Art, Smithsonian Institution, gift of John Gellatly; National Museum of Health and Medicine-AFIP 49007. **120:** Rijksmuseum, Amsterdam. **121:** Copyright The British Museum, London. **122, 123:** Amsterdams Historisch Museum (detail). **124:** Rijksmuseum, Amsterdam. **126:** Photo RMN, Paris-R. G. Ojeda. **129:** Rijksmuseum, Amsterdam. **131:** Artothek, Peissenberg/Mauritshuis, The Hague, *Anatomy Lesson* (detail) by Rembrandt van Rijn. **132:** Noortman (London) Ltd/Bridgeman Art Library, London. **133:** Victoria & Albert Museum, London/Bridgeman Art Library, London. **134:** Centraal Museum, Utrecht/Ernst Moritz. **136-139:** Border by John Drummond, © Time Life Inc., courtesy The Art Institute of Chicago. **136, 137:** Pieter Claesz (attrib. to), Dutch, 1597/98-1660, *Still Life* (detail), oil on panel, 1625/30, 48 x 76.9 cm, Simeon B. Williams Fund, 1935.300, photograph © 1999, The Art Institute of Chicago. All Rights Reserved. **138, 139:** Amsterdam School, *Preparations for a Feast* (detail), Birmingham Museums and Art Gallery, Birmingham, England; Mauritshuis, The Hague. **140, 141:** Frans Halsmuseum, Haarlem (detail). **142, 143:** Rijksmuseum, Amsterdam (detail). **144:** Schapowalow/Plessner, Hamburg. **145:** Centraalmuseum, Utrecht/Ernst Moritz. **146:** Artothek, Peissenberg/photo by Peter Willi, *The Lacemaker* (detail) by Jan Vermeer/Louvre, Paris. **147:** The Minneapolis Institute of Arts. **148, 149:** Amsterdams Historisch Museum. **150-157:** Background by John Drummond, © Time Life Inc. **150:** Staatliche Museen zu Berlin-Preussischer Kulturbesitz, Gemäldegalerie, photo by Jörg P. Anders (detail). **151:** Fine Arts Museums of San Francisco, gift of the Samuel H. Kress Foundation, 61.44.37. **152, 153:** Kimbell Art Museum, Fort Worth, Texas, Frans Hals, Dutch, 1581/85-1666, *The Rommel Pot Player* (detail) about 1618-22, oil on canvas 41-3/4 x 31-5/8"; Polesden Lacey, The McEwan Collection/National Trust Photographic Library, London (Derrick Witty); Museum van Loon, Amsterdam (detail). **154:** Staatliche Museen Kassel, Gemäldegalerie Alte Meister. **155:** Fitzwilliam Museum, University of Cambridge/Bridgeman Art Library, London. **156:** Photothèque des Musées de la Ville de Paris, cliché: Patrick Pierrain. **157:** Rijksmuseum, Amsterdam.

Design Elements: John Drummond, © Time Life Inc.; icon design by John Drummond, © Time Life Inc., courtesy Schapowalow.

BIBLIOGRAPHY

BOOKS

All the Paintings of the Rijksmuseum in Amsterdam. By the Department of Paintings of the Rijksmuseum. Amsterdam: Rijksmuseum, 1976.

Alpers, Svetlana. *Rembrandt's Enterprise: The Studio and the Market.* Chicago: University of Chicago Press, 1988.

Bailey, Anthony. *Rembrandt's House.* Boston: Houghton Mifflin, 1978.

Bailey, Martin. *Dürer.* London: Phaidon Press, 1995.

Bainton, Roland B.:
Here I Stand: A Life of Martin Luther. New York: Abingdon Press, 1950.
The Reformation of the Sixteenth Century. Boston: Beacon Press, 1952.
Women of the Reformation: In Germany and Italy. Minneapolis: Augsburg Publishing House, 1971.

Barbour, Violet. *Capitalism in Amsterdam in the 17th Century.* Ann Arbor: University of Michigan Press, 1950.

Benesch, Otto. *German Painting.* Geneva: Skira, 1966.

Bergendoff, Conrad, ed. *Luther's Works, Vol. 40.* Philadelphia: Muhlenberg Press, 1958.

Bertini, Giuseppe. *Le Nozze di Alessandro Farnese.* Milano: Skira, 1997.

Blickle, Peter. *The Revolution of 1525.* Trans. by Thomas A. Brady Jr. and H. C. Erik Midelfort. Baltimore: Johns Hopkins University Press, 1981.

Blok, P. *The Life of Admiral de Ruyter.* Trans. by G. J. Renier. Westport, Conn.: Greenwood Press, 1975.

Bonney, Richard. *The European Dynastic States, 1494-1660.* Oxford: Oxford University Press, 1991.

Boxer, C. R.:
The Dutch in Brazil, 1624-1654. Oxford: Clarendon Press, 1957.
The Dutch Seaborne Empire, 1600-1800. London: Hutchinson, 1965.

Brady, Thomas A., Jr. "Rites of Autonomy, Rites of Dependence." In *Religion and Culture in the Renaissance and Reformation.* Ed. by Steven Ozment. Kirksville, Mo.: Sixteenth Century Journal Publishers, 1989.

Brandi, Karl. *The Emperor Charles V.* London: Jonathan Cape, 1968.

Brecht, Martin.
Martin Luther: His Road to Reformation, 1483-1521, Vol. 1. Trans. by James L. Schaaf. Philadelphia, Fortress Press, 1985.
The Preservation of the Church, 1532-1546, Vol. 3.

Trans. by James L. Schaaf. Minneapolis: Fortress Press, 1993.
Shaping and Defining the Reformation, 1521-1532, Vol. 2. Trans. by James L. Schaaf. Minneapolis: Fortress Press, 1990.

Bromley, J. S., and E. H. Kossmann, eds. *Britain and the Netherlands.* London: Chatto & Windus, 1960.

Brown, Christopher, Jan Kelch, and Pieter van Thiel. *Rembrandt: The Master & His Workshop.* New Haven, Conn.: Yale University Press, 1991.

Burke, Peter. *Venice and Amsterdam.* Cambridge, England: Polity Press, 1994.

Cameron, Euan. *The European Reformation.* Oxford: Clarendon Press, 1991.

Chapman, H. Perry, et al. *Jan Steen: Painter and Storyteller.* Washington, D.C.: National Gallery of Art, 1996.

Christin, Olivier. *Les Réformes: Luther, Calvin et les Protestants.* Paris: Découvertes Gallimard, 1995.

Clasen, Claus-Peter. *Anabaptism: A Social History, 1525-1618.* Ithaca, N.Y.: Cornell University Press, 1972.

Columbia History of the World. New York: Harper & Row, 1972.

Crew, Phyllis Mack. *Calvinist Preaching and Iconoclasm in the Netherlands, 1544-1569.* Cambridge: Cambridge University Press, 1978.

Deursen, Arie Theodorus van. *Plain Lives in a Golden Age.* Trans. by Maarten Ultee. Cambridge: Cambridge University Press, 1991.

De Vries, Jan. *The Dutch Rural Economy in the Golden Age, 1500-1700.* New Haven, Conn.: Yale University Press, 1974.

Dixon, Laurinda S. *Perilous Chastity.* Ithaca, N.Y.: Cornell University Press, 1995.

Durant, Will. *The Reformation,* Vol. 6 of *The Story of Civilization.* New York: Simon and Schuster, 1957.

Durant, Will, and Ariel Durant. *The Story of Civilization:*
The Age of Louis XIV, Vol. 8. New York: Simon and Schuster, 1963.
The Age of Reason Begins, Vol. 7. New York: Simon and Schuster, 1961.

Dutch Art: An Encyclopedia. New York: Garland, 1997.

Dutch Brazil, Vol. 1. Rio de Janeiro: Editora Index, 1997.

Eells, Hastings. *The Attitude of Martin Bucer toward the Bigamy of Philip of Hesse.* New Haven, Conn.: Yale University Press, 1924.

Elton, G. R. *The New Cambridge Modern History, Vol. 2.* Cambridge: Cambridge University Press, 1962.

Encyclopedia of World Art. New York: McGraw-Hill, 1961.

Franits, Wayne E. *Paragons of Virtue.* Cambridge: Cambridge University Press, 1993.

Freedman, Luba. *Titian's Portraits through Aretino's Lens.* University Park: Pennsylvania State University Press, 1995.

Friedenthal, Richard. *Luther: His Life and Times.* Trans. by John Nowell. New York: Harcourt Brace Jovanovich, 1967.

Fruin, R. *The Siege and Relief of Leyden in 1574.* Trans. by Elizabeth Trevelyan. The Hague: Oxford University Press, 1927.

German Peasants' War. Ed. and trans. by Tom Scott and Bob Scribner. London: Humanities Press International, 1991.

German Peasant War of 1525. Ed. by Bob Scribner. London: George Allen & Unwin, 1979.

Germany: A New Social and Economic History, Vol. 1. Ed. by Bob Scribner. London: Arnold, 1996.

Geyl, Pieter. *The Revolt of the Netherlands, 1555-1609.* Totowa, N.J.: Barnes & Noble Books, 1958.

Gibson, Walter S. *Hieronymus Bosch.* London: Thames and Hudson, 1973.

Girouard, Mark. *Cities & People.* New Haven, Conn.: Yale University Press, 1985.

Goertz, Hans-Jürgen. *Thomas Müntzer.* Trans. by Jocelyn Jaquiery, ed. by Peter Matheson. Edinburgh: T&T Clark, 1993.

Gothic and Renaissance Art in Nuremberg. New York: Metropolitan Museum of Art, 1986.

Haak, Bob:
The Golden Age. Trans. by Elizabeth Willems-Treeman. New York: Harry N. Abrams, 1984.
Rembrandt. New York: Harry N. Abrams, 1969.

Haks, Donald, and Marie Christine van der Sman, eds. *Dutch Society in the Age of Vermeer.* Zwolle, Netherlands: Waanders, 1996.

Hale, J. R.:
Artists and Warfare in the Renaissance. New Haven, Conn.: Yale University Press, 1990.
The Civilization of Europe in the Renaissance. New York: Atheneum, 1994.
War and Society in Renaissance Europe, 1450-1620. Montreal: McGill-Queen's University Press, 1998.

Haley, K. H. D. *The Dutch in the Seventeenth Century.* New York: Harcourt Brace Jovanovich, 1972.

Health Care and Poor Relief in Protestant Europe, 1500-1700. Ed. by Ole Peter Grell and Andrew Cunningham. London: Routledge, 1997.

Heckscher, William S. *Rembrandt's Anatomy of Dr. Nicolaas Tulp.* New York: New York University Press, 1958.

Hillerbrand, Hans J.:
Landgrave Philipp of Hesse, 1504-1567. St. Louis: Foundation for Reformation Research, 1967.
The Reformation. New York: Harper & Row, 1964.

Holborn, Hajo. *A History of Modern Germany.* Princeton, N.J.: Princeton University Press, 1959.

Holmes, George. *Renaissance.* New York: St. Martin's Press, 1996.

Hsia, R. Po-chia. *Society and Religion in Münster.* New Haven, Conn.: Yale University Press, 1984.

Hutchison, Jane Campbell. *Albrecht Dürer: A Biography.* Princeton, N.J.: Princeton University Press, 1990.

Israel, Jonathan I.:
Dutch Primacy in World Trade, 1585-1740. Oxford, England: Clarendon Press, 1989.
The Dutch Republic: Its Rise, Greatness, and Fall, 1477-1806. Oxford, England: Clarendon Press, 1995.

Janson, H. W. *History of Art.* New York: Harry N. Abrams, 1968.

Johannes Vermeer. Washington, D.C.: National Gallery of Art, 1995.

Judith Leyster: A Dutch Master and Her World. Worcester, Mass.: Worcester Art Museum, 1993.

Kistemaker, Renee, and Roelof van Gelder. *Amsterdam.* New York: Abbeville Press, 1982.

Kitchen, Martin. *The Cambridge Illustrated History of Germany.* Cambridge: Cambridge University Press, 1996.

Lambert, Audrey M. *The Making of the Dutch Landscape.* London: Academic Press, 1985.

Luther, Martin. *Luther's Works:*
Career of the Reformer, Vol. 31. Ed. by Harold J. Grimm. Philadelphia: Muhlenberg Press, 1957.
Table Talk, Vol. 54. Ed. and trans. by Theodore G. Tappert. Philadelphia: Fortress Press, 1967.

McGrath, Alister E. *Reformation Thought.* Oxford: Blackwell, 1993.

McKay, John P., Bennett D. Hill, and John Buckler. *A History of World Societies.* Boston: Houghton Mifflin, 1992.

Manchester, William. *A World Lit Only by Fire: The Medieval Mind and the Renaissance.* Boston: Little, Brown, 1992.

Midelfort, H. C. Erik. *Mad Princes of Renaissance Germany.* Charlottesville: University Press of Virginia, 1994.

Motley, John Lothrop. *The Rise of the Dutch Republic* (5 vols.). New York: Harper and Brothers, 1900.

Muller, Sheila D. *Charity in the Dutch Republic.* Ann Arbor, Mich.: UMI Research Press, 1985.

Murray, John J. *Amsterdam in the Age of Rembrandt.* University of Oklahoma Press, 1967.

Musper, H. T. *Albrecht Dürer.* New York: Harry N. Abrams, 1966.

Nauert, Charles G., Jr. *Humanism and the Culture of Renaissance Europe.* Cambridge: Cambridge University Press, 1995.

North, Michael. *Art and Commerce in the Dutch Golden Age.* Trans. by Catherine Hill. New Haven, Conn.: Yale University Press, 1997.

Oberman, Heiko A. *Luther: Man between God and the Devil.* Trans. by Eileen Walliser-Schwarzbart. New Haven, Conn.: Yale University Press, 1989.

Oman, Charles. *A History of the Art of War in the Sixteenth Century.* New York: E. P. Dutton and Co., 1937.

Origins of Museums. Ed. by Oliver Impey and Arthur MacGregor. Oxford: Clarendon Press, 1985.

Oxford Encyclopedia of the Reformation (4 vols.). New York: Oxford University Press, 1996.

Oxford Illustrated History of the Crusades. Ed. by Jonathan Riley-Smith. Oxford: Oxford University Press, 1995.

Ozment, Steven:
The Age of Reform. New Haven, Conn.: Yale University Press, 1980.
Protestants. New York: Doubleday, 1992.
Three Behaim Boys. New Haven, Conn.: Yale University Press, 1990.
When Fathers Ruled. Cambridge, Mass.: Harvard University Press, 1983.

Panofsky, Erwin. *The Life and Art of Albrecht Dürer.* Princeton, N.J.: Princeton University Press, 1955.

Parker, Geoffrey, and Allen Lane. *The Dutch Revolt.* London: Penguin Books, 1977.

Pavord, Anna. *The Tulip.* New York: Bloomsbury, 1999.

Postma, Johannes Menne. *The Dutch in the Atlantic Slave Trade, 1600-1815.* Cambridge: Cambridge University Press, 1990.

Prinz, Wolfram. *Dürer.* New York: Smithmark, 1998.

Putnam, Ruth. *William the Silent,* Vols. 1 and 2. New York: G. P. Putnam's Sons, 1895.

Regin, Deric. *Traders, Artists, Burghers: A Cultural History of Amsterdam in the 17th Century.* Amsterdam: Van Gorcum, Assan, 1976.

Renaissance and Reformation in Germany. Ed. by Gerhart Hoffmeister. New York: Frederick Ungar, 1977.

Reu, Johann Michael. *The Augsburg Confession.* Chicago: Wartburg Publishing House, 1930.

Rijksmuseum Amsterdam: Highlights from the Collection. Amsterdam: Rijksmuseum, 1995.

Riley, Gilliam. *The Dutch Table: Gastronomy in the Golden Age of the Netherlands.* San Francisco: Pomegranate Artbooks, 1994.

Roosbroeck, R. Van. *Willem de Zwijger.* Antwerp: Mercatorfonds, 1974.

Roots of Western Civilization:
Crafts and Trade, Vol. 3. Danbury, Conn.: Grolier Educational, 1994.
Rural Landscapes, Vol. 9. Danbury, Conn.: Grolier Educational, 1994.

Roper, Lyndal. *The Holy Household: Women and Morals, in Reformation Augsburg.* Oxford, England: Clarendon Press, 1989.

Rowen, Herbert H. *The Princes of Orange.* Cambridge: Cambridge University Press, 1988.

Rowlands, John. *Hieronymus Bosch: The Garden of Earthly Delights.* Oxford, England: Phaidon, 1979.

Rupp, Gordon. *Patterns of Reformation.* Philadelphia: Fortress Press, 1969.

Russell, Francis, and the Editors of Time-Life Books. *The World of Dürer, 1471-1528* (Time-Life Library of Art series). New York: Time, 1967.

Sastrow, Bartholomew. *Social Germany in Luther's Time.* Westminster: Archibald Constable, 1902.

Schade, Werner. *Cranach: A Family of Master Painters.* Trans. by Helen Sebba. New York: Putnam, 1980.

Schama, Simon. *The Embarrassment of Riches.* New York: Vintage, 1987.

Schupbach, William. *The Paradox of Rembrandt's 'Anatomy of Dr. Tulp.'* London: Wellcome Institute for the History of Medicine, 1982.

Schwartz, Gary. *Rembrandt: His Life, His Paintings.* New York: Viking, 1985.

Schwiebert, E. G. *Luther and His Times.* St. Louis: Concordia, 1950.

Scribner, R. W. *For the Sake of Simple Folk.* Cambridge: Cambridge University Press, 1981.

Sellin, Johan Thorsten. *Pioneering in Penology.* Philadelphia: University of Pennsylvania Press, 1944.

Simon, Edith, and the Editors of Time-Life. *The Reformation* (Great Ages of Man series). New York: Time-Life, 1966.

Slive, Seymour. *Frans Hals.* London: Royal Academy of Arts, 1989.

Slive, Seymour, and H. R. Hoetink. *Jacob van Ruisdael.* New York: Abbeville Press, 1981.

Smith, Jeffrey Chipps. *Nuremberg: A Renaissance City, 1500-1618.* Austin: University of Texas Press, 1983.

Spitz, Lewis W. *The Protestant Reformation, 1517-1559.* New York: Harper & Row, 1985.

Stone-Ferrier, Linda A. *Dutch Prints of Daily Life: Mirrors of Life or Masks of Morals?* Lawrence, Kans.: Spencer Museum of Art, 1983.

Strauss, Gerald. *Sixteenth-Century Germany: Its Topography and Topographers.* Madison: University of Wisconsin Press, 1959.

Strauss, Gerald, trans. *Manifestations of Discontent in Germany on the Eve of the Reformation.* Bloomington: Indiana University Press, 1971.

Strauss, Walter L., ed. *Max Geisberg: The German Single-Leaf Woodcut, 1500-1550.* New York: Hacker Art Books, 1974.

Strien, C. D. van. *British Travellers in Holland during the Stuart Period.* New York: E. J. Brill, 1993.

Sutton, Peter C. *Pieter de Hooch: 1629-1684.* New Haven, Conn.: Yale University Press, 1998.

Swart, K. W. *William the Silent and the Revolt of the Netherlands.* London: Historical Association, 1978.

Tanis, James, and Daniel Horst. *Images of Discord: A Graphic Interpretation of the Opening Decades of the Eighty Years' War.* Bryn Mawr, Pa.: Bryn Mawr College Library, 1993.

Thompson, Bard. *Humanists and Reformers: A History of the Renaissance and Reformation.* Grand Rapids: William B. Eerdmans, 1996.

Thornton, Peter:
Authentic Decor: The Domestic Interior, 1620-1920. New York: Viking, 1984.
Seventeenth-Century Interior Decoration in England, France and Holland. New Haven, Conn.: Yale University Press, 1978.

Voet, Leon. *Antwerp: The Golden Age.* Antwerp: Mercatorfonds, 1973.

Wallace, Robert, and the Editors of Time-Life Books. *The World of Rembrandt, 1606-1669* (Time-Life Library of Art series). New York: Time, 1968.

Wedgwood, C.V. *William the Silent.* London: Jonathan Cape, 1967.

Westermann, Mariët:
The Amusements of Jan Steen: Comic Painting in the Seventeenth Century. Zwolle, Netherlands: Waanders, 1997.
A Worldly Art: The Dutch Republic, 1585-1718. New York: Harry N. Abrams, 1996.

Wheatcroft, Andrew. *The Habsburgs.* London: Viking, 1995.

Wheelock, Arthur K., Jr. *A Collector's Cabinet.* Washington, D.C.: National Gallery of Art, 1998.

White, Christopher. *Rembrandt.* New York: Thames and Hudson, 1984.

Wiesner, Merry E. *Working Women in Renaissance Germany.* New Brunswick, N.J.: Rutgers University Press, 1986.

Wilckens, Leonie von. *Mansions in Miniature: Four Centuries of Dolls' Houses.* New York: Viking Press, 1978.

Wilson, Charles. *The Dutch Republic: And the Civilisation of the Seventeenth Century.* New York: McGraw-Hill, 1968.

Witte, John, Jr. *From Sacrament to Contract: Marriage, Religion, and Law in the Western Tradition.* Louisville, Ky.: Westminster John Knox Press, 1997.

Wright, William John. *Capitalism, the State, and the Lutheran Reformation: Sixteenth-Century Hesse.* Athens: Ohio University Press, 1988.

Wunder, Heide. *He Is the Sun, She Is the Moon.* Trans. by Thomas Dunlap. Cambridge, Mass.: Harvard University Press, 1998.

Zumthor, Paul. *Daily Life in Rembrandt's Holland.* Trans. by Simon Watson Taylor. Stanford, Calif.: Stanford University Press, 1994.

PERIODICALS
Art Bulletin, September 1989.

Barker, Paula S. Datsko. "Caritas Pirckheimer: A Female Humanist Confronts the Reformation." *The Sixteenth Century Journal,* Summer 1995.

Ozment, Steven. "The Private Life of an Early Modern Teenager: A Nuremberg Lutheran Visits Catholic Louvain (1577)." *Journal of Family History,* January 1996.

OTHER SOURCES
Bussmann, Klaus, and Heinz Schilling, eds. *1648: War and Peace in Europe.* Exhibition catalog. Münster/Osnabrück: 26th Exhibition of the Council of Europe, October 24, 1998-January 17, 1999.

INDEX

Page numbers in italics refer to illustrations or illustrated text.

A
"Abduction of Europa, The" (Dürer), *57*

Adriaanszoon, Adriaan: dissection of, 130, *131*

Agriculture: Dutch, *81, 100-101*

Albrecht of Brandenburg, 25

Aleander (papal nuncio): quoted, 36

All Saints' Foundation, Wittenberg: saints' relics, 27-28

Almshouse: Dutch, *134-135*

Alva, duke of (Spanish general), 89, 90, 91, 92

Amsdorf, Nikolaus von, 41

Amsterdam, Netherlands: anatomy, public, 130, *131;* Behaim in, 125-127; building boom, 111; coopers guild officers, *106;* Dam Square, *148-149;* as financial center, 106, *107;* government, 133, 134, 135, 136; harbor, *98-99;* ice, social life on, *122-123;* migration to, 110-112; power wielded by, 133-134; Ruyter, Michiel and Anna de, in, 141, 143, 146-148; spinning house, 127; street life, *120, 121;* theater, 134; Tulp's role in, 130-133, *131,* 134-135, 136, 140; waterway, *111. See also* Rembrandt van Rijn

Anabaptists (Christian sectarians), *68*

Anatomies: public, 128, 130, *131*

Anatomy Lesson, The (Rembrandt), 130, *131*

Anna (Philip of Hesse's mother), 64

Anna of Saxony (William's wife), 85, 90

Antwerp, Netherlands, 99; hedge preaching outside, *88;* unrest in, 87, 89-90

Apocalypse (Dürer): woodcut from, *58*

Arctic: Dutch whaling, *102-103*

Army: supply train, *76-77. See also* War

Art: buyers, 114-*115;* propaganda, 37-39; students, 112-113, *114-115,* 116, 120, *155. See also* names of artists

Augsburg, Germany: Charles V's welcome, 69-70, *70-71;* diet, 71; Luther's hearing in, 15, *20-21,* 20-22

Augsburg Confession (1530), 70; reading of, *71*

Augustine, Saint: quoted, 31

B
Bagpipers, *82, 126*

Baldinucci, Filippo: quoted, 110

Banks and banking: Amsterdam Exchange Bank, 106; Fugger family, 25

Banquets: Dutch, *136-137, 138*

Baptism: by layman, 34

Barlaeus, Caspar, 112; delusions, 132; quoted, 111, 131

Bathsheba with King David's Letter (Rembrandt), 122

Bedwarmer, *133*

Beeldenstorm (riots), 87-88, *89*

Beer: supply for Dutch wedding, *82*

Beggars (Dutch rebels), 86, 87, 88; Sea Beggars, 90-91, *92-93, 94-95,* 96

Beggar's bowl: crafted by artisan, *87*

Behaim, Stephan Carl, 125-128

Bigamy: Philip of Hesse's, 72-73

Bird-shaped ewer, *118*

Black Cloister, Wittenberg: Luthers in, 46, 48

Blankaart, Stephanus, 150

Boats, Dutch: Amsterdam harbor, *98-99;* herring fleet, 102; Leiden relief, *94-95;* waterways with, *100-101, 129*

Bonfire: Wittenberg, 34–*35*

Book burning, 34, *35*

Bora, Katherine von, *51;* enterprises, 48, 50; marriage to Luther, 46-48

Bosch, Hieronymus: art by, *18*

Bourse (building), Amsterdam, 106, *107*

Bowmen's Bastion moat, Amsterdam, *111*

Braa, Abraham de, 125, 127, 128

Brazil: Behaim in, 128; slaves, *105*

Breast-feeding, 47, 150, *151*

Breestraat (street), Amsterdam: Rembrandt's house on, 110, 116

Brill, The, Netherlands: Sea Beggars' taking of, 91, *92-93*

Brueghel, Pieter, the Younger: art by, *80-83; 100, 101*

Bull, papal (1520), 32; burning, 34–*35*

Burgomasters: Amsterdam, 133, 134, 135, 136

Bursas (residential colleges), 29-30

C

Cajetan of Thiene, Cardinal: Luther's meeting with, *20-21,* 20-22

Calvin, John, 74, *75*

Calvinists, 10, *75;* churches sacked by, 87-88, *89;* hedge preaching, 87, *88;* Philip II's crusade against, 84, 86, 88, 90; Tulp as, 134, 135; William as, 92

Cardinals: Cajetan, 20-22, *21;* cartoon of, *38*

Casimir, Prince (Brandenburg), 69

Castle church, Wittenberg, 27; Karlstadt's service in, 42; Luther at, *16,* 17; saints' relics, 27-28

Castles, 41, 42, *43*

Catholic Church: and Fuggers, 25; holidays, Dutch, 135-136, *156-157;* indulgence sales, 16-17, *19,* 21; nun with monk, *30;* saints' relics, 27-28

Cattle raising: Netherlands, *100-101*

Charles V, Holy Roman Emperor, 9, 34, 35, 64, 72, 78; abdication, 80; Augsburg welcome, 69-70, *70-71;*

and Fuggers, 25; imperial ban (Edict of Worms), 42, 44, 45; Mühlberg victory, *78-79;* and Protestants, 70, 71, 73, 77, 78, 79, 80; Sastrow's observation of, 74, 76; son compared to, 79-80; at Worms, 36, 39-40

Charlotte of Bourbon, 96

Chiaroscuro: Rembrandt's use of, 113

Children, 47, *120, 150-157;* baptism, *34;* with *kolf* sticks, *144, 152-153, 157;* with pancakes, *82, 120;* de Ruyter family, *143;* table manners, *49*

Chinese collectibles, *119*

Christ: Dürer's portrayal of self as, *60;* pope contrasted with, *38;* Rembrandt's paintings of, 109, 110

Christina of Saxony, 71, *72*

Churches: Anabaptists' corpses in, *68;* Calvinist sacking of, 87-88, *89;* Calvinists in, *75;* Luther preaching in, *40-41;* village, *26-27. See also* Castle church

Cocq, Frans Banning, 115

Coins: minting of, *24;* Roman, *119*

Collectors' cabinets, 116, *117;* items in, *118-119;* miniature, *145*

Communion: at Karlstadt's service, 42

Coopers guild officers: Amsterdam, *106*

Council of Konstanz: Hus at, 15, 40

Council of Troubles, 90

Cranach, Lucas, 27, 46-47; woodcuts, *38*

D

Dam Square, Amsterdam, *148-149*

Dancers and dancing: Dutch, *83, 85, 126*

Delft, Netherlands: William in, *96-97*

Devil: and Luther, *29;* and witch burning, *28-29*

Dikes: cutting of, 93; use of, 101

Dircx, Geertge, 121-122

Dishes: banquet, *136-137;* Chinese, *119*

Dissections, 128, 130, *131*

Dollhouse, *145*

Domestic servants, 50, *147*

Dominicans: Cajetan, 20-22, *21;* Eck, Johann, 31; Tetzel, Johann, 19

Dressing table: lady at, *147*

Drinking: celebrations, *82-83;* establishments for, *126*-127; family, *138-*

139; monk and nun, *30;* Rembrandt, *112*

Dürer, Albrecht, *52, 55, 60,* 116; Luther admired by, 41, 61; works by, *52-61*

Dutch (people). *See* Netherlands

Dutch East India Company, 105, 125; trading depot, *104-105*

Dutch West India Company, 105, 125; Behaim in, 127-128

Dutchwomen: in arts, 146; Behaim and, 127; benefactress, *134-135;* in business, 145; conviviality, *82-83, 138-139;* with doctor, *132;* food preparation, 80, *138;* housework, *144*-145; lacemaker, *146;* marketing, *102,* 146-148; mothers, 150, *151;* musicians, *108-109, 126;* pancake vendor, *120;* Rembrandt and, *112,* 113-114, 121-124; Ruyter, Anna de, *141-142,* 143, 144, 146-148, *149;* in spinning house, 127; toilet, *147*

E

East India Company, Dutch, 105, 125; trading depot, *104-105*

Eck, Johann: Luther's debate with, 31

Edict of Worms (1521), 42, 44, 45

Education, *154,* 155; art, *112-113, 114-115,* 116, 120, *155;* Luther's, 29-30; Rembrandt's, 112-113

Egmont, Count, 88-89, 90

Elisabeth (Philip's sister), 72, 73

Employment agents, 50

Engelhardt, Simeon, 74

English-Dutch wars, 11, 135, 140, 148

Erasmus, Desiderius, *23,* 45, 61

Erfurt, Germany, 29; bull published in, 32; Luther in, 29-30, 36

Eternal League of God (rebel army), 68

Evelyn, John: quoted, 114

Exsurge Domine (papal bull; 1520), 32; burning of, 34–*35*

F

Farming: Dutch, *81, 100-101*

Feasts: Dutch, *136-137,* 138

Festivals and holidays: Dutch, *82-83,* 135-136, *156-157*

Fish and fishing, *102-103;* on ice, *122*

Flemish celebration, *82-83*

Fluits (Dutch cargo ships), *99*

Food supply, Dutch, *136-139;* agricul-

ture, *81, 100-101;* charitable distribution, *134-135;* fishing industry, *102-103;* Leiden relief, *94-95;* peasants and, *80,* 81, 82

Foot warmers: women with, *138-139, 151*

"Four Apostles, The" (Dürer), *61*

France: vs. Netherlands, 11, 140, 141, 148; Protestants, 75, *91*

Frankenhausen, Germany: in Peasants' War, 68-69

Frederick Henry, Prince (Orange), 110

Frederick the Wise (elector of Saxony), 17, 27-28; dream, *16-17;* and Luther, 16, 20, 28, 35, 41, 44; Müntzer's appeal to, 51

Friederich, Lucas: correspondence, 125, 127, 128

Fugger, Jacob, 25

Fugger family, 20, *25*

G

Genevan Reformation, 74

George, Duke (Saxony), 42, 46, 69

George, Margrave (Brandenburg), 70

Gérard, Balthazar, 96-97

Germany, 8-9; Anabaptists, *68;* castle church (Wittenberg), *16,* 17, 27-28, 42; Charles V's welcome back to, 69-70, *70-71;* cities, scenery of, 25, 27, 29; coins, minting of, *24;* defeat of Charles V, 80; defeat of Protestants, *78-79;* diets in, 36, 39, 69, *71;* Dürer in, 54, 59; electoral states, 22, 24; Fugger family, 20, *25;* hunters, *64-65;* knights, imperial, 31, 41-42, *44;* maps, *12-13;* peasants, *64,* 65-69, *67;* pope resented in, 24; Sastrows in, 73-74, 76-77, 78-80; village, *26-27;* William's exile in, 90; women's work, 50-51. *See also* Luther, Martin; Philip of Hesse

Grain, Dutch: charitable distribution, *134-135;* harvesters, *100, 101*

Great Piece of Turf (Dürer), *56*

Guilds, Amsterdam, 106, 130, *131*

Guitar: decorated, *118-119*

H

Haarlem, Netherlands: conquest, *62-63*

Hals, Frans: portrait by, *150*

Harlem (ship): Behaim on, 127-128

Hedge preaching, 87, *88*

Helfenstein, Ludwig von (Count of

Weinsberg), 66-67
Hell: Bosch's vision of, *18*
Herring industry: Dutch, 102, *103*
Hesse (state), Germany: peasant attack, *67;* vs. peasant rebels, 68-69
Holbein, Hans, the Younger: art by, *23*
Holidays and festivals: Dutch, *82-83,* 135-136, *156-157*
Holland. *See* Netherlands
Holy Roman Empire, 15-16, 22, 24
Hooch, Pieter de: art by, *151*
Huguenots (French Protestants), 91
Huik (cloak), 146
Hunters, *64-65, 80;* Luther with, *42*
Hus, Jan, 15, 16, 40; burning of, *16*
Hutten, Ulrich von, 31, 41-42, *44*
Huygens, Constantijn, 110, 112, 113, 149

I

IJ (sea inlet), Amsterdam, *122-123*
India: Dutch trading depot, *104-105*
Indulgences: sale of, 16-17, *19,* 21
Infants, 150, *156;* baptism, *34;* breast-feeding of, *47,* 150, *151*
Inns and taverns, *126-127*
Italy: in dream, *16-17;* Dürer's travels, 52, 57; Sastrow's travels, 77-78

J

Jaureguy, Juan, 96
Jesus. *See* Christ
John (elector of Saxony), 48, 51, 70
John, Saint, *61*
John Frederick (elector of Saxony), 79, 80
John of Leiden: execution, 68
Jörg, Junker: Luther's identity, *14-15,* 41, 44

K

Karlstadt, Andreas, 22, 31, 42, 45
Kermis (Dutch celebration), *82-83*
Kettenbach, Heinrich von: quoted, 38
Knights, imperial, 31, 41-42, *44;* Luther's disguise as, *14-15,* 41, 44
Knights' War (1523), 64
Koberger, Anton, 59
Kolf sticks, *123, 144, 152-153, 157*
Koppe, Leonhard, 46, 48

L

Lacemaker, *146*
Lacquerware: Chinese, *119*
Lastman, Pieter, 113
Learned Maid, The (Schurman), 146

Leiden, Netherlands: relief of, *94-95;* Rembrandt in, 112, 113; siege of, 92-94, 96
Leo X, Pope, 21; bull, 32, 34-35; dream representing, *16-17*
Letter to the Princes of Saxony concerning the Rebellious Spirit (Luther), 51
Leyster, Judith, 146
Lievens, Jan, 113
Linen chest: women with, *144*
Louis, Count (Nassau), 86, 90, 91-92
Louis XIV, King (France), 140
Low Countries. *See* Netherlands
Luther, Hans, 28-29, 30-31
Luther, Margarete, 28-29
Luther, Martin, 8, 15-51; abduction, planned, 40-41; Augsburg hearing, 15, *20-21,* 20-22; bonfire arranged by, *34-35;* children, 47; cloister departures aided by, 45-46; death of, 77; devil and, *29;* in disguise as knight, *14-15,* 41, 44; and Dürer, 41, 61; Eck's debate with, 31; under Edict of Worms, 42, 44, 45; and Erasmus, 23; Erfurt education, 29-30; financial problems, 48; Frederick's dream about, *16-17;* Frederick's support of, 16, 20, 28, 35; indulgence sales opposed by, 16-17, 19, 21; influence over others, 31; marriage, view of, 46; marriage of, 46-48; and Melanchthon, 31, 70; monastic life, beginning of, 30; vs. Müntzer, 51; and Ninety-five Theses, *16-17;* order restored by, 44-45; papal bull threatening, 32, 34-35; parents, 28-29, 30-31; patriotic view of, 31, 36, 45; and Philip of Hesse's marriage, 72, 73; as preacher, 31, 36, *40-41,* 44; on printed communication, 38, 45; propaganda portrayals of, *37;* publications, 32-34; return from exile, 42, 44; saints' words influencing, 31; and Sastrows, 73-74; and Twelve Articles, 66; Wartburg as refuge for, 41, 42, *43;* wife, 46-48, 50, *51;* in Worms, 36, 39-40
Lutheranism: Augsburg Confession, 70, 71; Philip of Hesse as convert, 63, 69
Lyon, France: Calvinist congregation, 75

M

Maps, 12-13
Margaret of Parma (regent), 84, *86,* 87,

88, 89, 90; son's wedding ball, 85
Margaret of Saale, 72-73
Mark, Saint, *61*
Markets: fish, *102;* trip to, 146-148; Wittenberg, 27
Marriage: Luther's view of, 46. *See also* Wedding festivities
Maurice, Duke (Saxony), 78, 79, 80
Maximilian I, Holy Roman Emperor, 20, 64; succession question, 31, 34
Medicine, 128, 130-133, *131, 132*
Melanchthon, Philipp, 31, 42; Augsburg Confession, 70; baptism by, *34;* bonfire publicized by, 34; booklet by, woodcuts from, *38;* and Philip of Hesse, 63, 72, 73
Melencolia I (Dürer), *59*
Memmingen, Germany: peasant alliance, 66
Mental illness: Tulp's cases, 132
Mercenaries: Italian, 77
Microscope: decorated, *119*
Military: supplies, 76-77. *See also* War
Moat: Amsterdam, *111*
Monks: departure from cloister, 45-46; with nun, *30;* peasant attack on, 67. *See also* Luther, Martin
Mühlberg, Battle of (1547), 78-79
Mühlhausen, Germany: in Peasants' War, 67-68, 69
Münster, Germany: Anabaptists, *68*
Müntzer, Thomas, 45, 51, 67-69
Musicians and musical instruments: bagpipers, *82, 126;* family, *140-141;* guitar, *118-119;* at inn, *126;* virginal, *108-109;* wedding procession, *26-27*
Musicos (drinking halls), 127

N

Naval engagements: de Ruyter as hero, 141, *142-143,* 148-149; Sea Beggars, 90-91, *92-93, 94-95,* 96
Netherlands and Netherlanders, 8-11; agriculture, *81, 100-101;* Antwerp unrest, 87; art buyers, *114-115;* art students, 112-113, *114-115,* 116, 120, *155;* Bosch, art by, *18;* The Brill, taking of, 91, *92-93;* charity, *134-135;* children, *82, 120, 139, 143, 144, 150-157;* collectors' cabinets, 116, *117-119, 145;* dollhouse, *145;* English conflicts with, 11, 135, 140, 148; festivals and holidays, *82-83,* 135-136, *156-157;* fishing in-

dustry, *102-103;* France vs., 11, 140, 141, 148; Leiden siege and relief, 92-94, *94-95,* 96; maps, 12-13; meals, *136-139;* medicine, 128, 130-133, *131, 132;* musicians, *82, 108-109, 126, 140-141;* peasants, *80-83, 100, 101;* political system, 84; regent (Margaret of Parma), 84, *86,* 87, 88, 89, 90; de Ruyter family, 141-144, *142-143,* 146-149; vs. Spaniards, 10, *62-63,* 89, 90, 91, *92-93,* 94, 96, 142; as trading empire, *98-99, 104-105;* tulipomania, 125; wedding ball, *85;* windmills, use of, *100-101, 129. See also* Amsterdam; Calvinists; Dutchwomen; Philip II; Rembrandt van Rijn; William, Prince
Ninety-five Theses (Luther), 17; dream about, *16-17*
Northern Company: whaling, *102-103*
Noozeman, Ariane, 146
Nuns and monks, *30;* departure of, 45-46
Nürnberg, Germany: Dürer in, 54

P

Pancakes, *82, 120*
Passional Christi und Antichristi (Cranach and Melanchthon), *38*
Paul, Saint, *61;* influence on Luther, 31
Peasants, *80-83;* agriculture, *81, 100-101;* burdens on, 64, 65-66; revolt, 66-69, *67*
Peasants' War (mid-1520s), 66-69, *67*
Pentecost: Netherlands, *156*
Peter, Saint, *61*
Pewter: Dutch tableware, *136-137*
Philip II, King (Spain), 9-10, 79-80, 84; Alva's efforts for, *62-63,* 89, 90, 91, 92; bounty on William by, 96; riots, reaction to, 88; William's break with, 84, 85-86
Philip of Hesse, 63-64, *73;* in Augsburg, 69, 70; defeat of, 79; freeing of, 80; as Lutheran convert, 63, 69; and peasants, 65, 67, 69; and Schmalkaldic League, 71, 73; wives, 71-73, *72*
Pirates: vs. Dutch, 142, 143
Polders: Netherlands, *100-101*
Pope, 21; bull, 32, 34-35; dream representing, *16-17;* German resentment of, 24; and indulgence sales, *19,* 21; Leipzig debate about, 31; propaganda portrayals of, *38, 39*

"Praying Hands, The" (Dürer), *53*
Printer's workshop, *33*
Propaganda: printed, *37-39*
Protestant Reformation, 25; Anabaptists, *68;* in Augsburg, 70; baptism by layman, *34;* Calvin, John, 74, *75;* conditions fostering, 24; defeat of Charles V, 80; Dürer's affinity with, 61; Huguenots, 91; Müntzer in, 45, 51, 68-69; Philip of Hesse's conversion, 63, 69; propaganda, printed, *37-39;* Reformed church, Feast of St. Nicholas opposed by, 135-136; Reformed church, Stoffels and, 123; Schmalkaldic League, 9, 71, 73, *78-79;* spread of, 45; upheavals in Wittenberg, 42, 44. *See also* Calvinists; Luther, Martin
Purgatory: and indulgences, 16, 17, 19

R

Rakes: Dutch peasants with, *81*
Ratcatcher: Amsterdam, *121*
Reformation. *See* Luther, Martin; Protestant Reformation
Relics, saints': Wittenberg, 27-28
Religion: pagan elements, 29; village church, *26-27. See also* Catholic Church; Protestant Reformation
Rembrandt van Rijn, 109-110, 112-114, 115-116; *The Anatomy Lesson,* 130, *131;* Breestraat house, 110, 116; Christ's Passion series, 109, 110; city life depicted by, *120, 121;* in countryside, 120; and Dircx, 121-122; education, 112-113; establishment in profession, 113; financial problems, 124; and Huygens, 110, 113; patrons, 110; self-portraits, *112,* 115-116, 125; son, Titus, 121, 123, 124-125; and Stoffels, 121, 122-124; as teacher, 116, 120; wife, Saskia, *112,* 113-114, 121; and Wtenbogaert, 109, 110
Resurrection of Christ, The (Rembrandt), 109, 110
Rhine River, Europe, *129*
Roman Empire: currency, *119*
Rome, Italy: dream about, *16-17;* Sastrow's trip to, 77
Rommel pot: man playing, *152*

Ruysch, Frederick, 116
Ruyter, Anna de, 141-*142,* 143, 144, 146-148, 149; family, *142-143*
Ruyter, Michiel de, 141, *142*-144, 147-149; family, *142-143*

S

Sachs, Hans: etiquette rules by, 49
Sacraments: baptism, *34;* Communion, 42; Luther's views of, 34
Saint Nicholas, Feast of: Netherlands, 135-136, 156, *157*
St. Peter's basilica, Rome, 17
Saints' relics: Wittenberg, 27-28
Salvation: Luther's views, 17, 31
Sastrow, Bartholomew, 73-74, 76-80; history witnessed by, 76, 79-80; jobs, 74, 76-77, 78; travels, 73, 77-78
Sastrow, John, 73-74, 76, 77
Saxony (state), Germany, 22, 24, 46, 68-69. *See also* Wittenberg
Schmalkaldic League, 9, 71, 73; defeat of, *78-79*
Schmalkaldic War (1546-1547), 77, *78-79*
Schooling. *See* Education
Schurman, Anna Maria van, 146
Schwartz, Matthaus, *25;* art by, *25*
Sea Beggars (Dutch rebels), 90-91; The Brill, taking of, 91, *92-93;* Leiden rescue, *94-95*
Serfdom: end to, peasants' demand for, 66; in Netherlands, 81
Ships: *fluits, 99; Harlem,* Behaim on, 127-128; herring fleet, 102; merchant, *98-99, 104-105;* Sea Beggars, 90-91, *92-93;* whaling, *102-103*
Shoemaker's shop, *50-51*
Sickingen, Franz von, 31
Sigmund, von Lupfen, count (Stülingen), 65
Silver: coins, minting of, *24*
Six, Jan, 120
Slaves: Brazil, *105*
Spalatin, Georg, 20, 28, 31, 48
Spaniards: vs. Dutch, 10, *62-63,* 89, 90, 91, *92-93,* 94, 96, 142; vs. France, 140
Speyer, Germany: diets, 69; Sastrow in, 74, 76, 79
Spinning house: Amsterdam, 127

Spitsbergen (island), Arctic Ocean: Dutch whaling, *102-103*
Stock exchange: Amsterdam, 106, *107*
Stoffels, Hendrickje, 121, 122-124
Stör, Caspar, 128
Stühlingen, Germany: peasants, 65
Sugar mill: Brazil, *105*
Surgeons guild: Amsterdam, 130, *131*
Swabia (duchy), Germany: peasants, 66
Switzerland: Calvin in, 74; Hutten in, 45

T

Table manners: children's, 49
Table setting: Dutch feast, *136-137*
Taverns and inns, *126-127*
Tenth Penny (tax), 91
Tetzel, Johann, 19
Theater: Amsterdam, 134
Titian (Italian painter): art by, *78*
Trade: Dutch, *98-99, 104-105*
Trip brothers: homes, *111*
Tulips: mania for, 125; still life with, *124;* as Tulp's trademark, 131
Tulp, Nicolaes: celebration for, 136, 140; medical career, 130-133, *131;* political career, 133, 134-135, 136
Twelve Articles (document), 66

U

Urine: examination of, *132*
Uylenburgh, Hendrik, 113
Uylenburgh, Saskia van, *112,* 113-114, 121

V

Venice, Italy: Dürer in, 57
Village scene: Germany, *26-27*
Virginal (musical instrument), *108-109*
Viterbo, Italy: Sastrow in, 77-78
Volbergen (Frederick Henry's paymaster), 110
Vondel, Joost van den, 134

W

War: Dutch-Anglo, 11, 135, 140, 148; France vs. Netherlands, 11, 140, 141, 148; Huguenots in, 91; Knights' War, 64; Leiden, siege and relief of, 92-94, *94-95,* 96; Peasants' War, 66-69, *67;* Schmalkaldic War, 77, *78-79;*

Sea Beggars' role, 91, *92-93, 94-95,* 96; Spanish involvement, 10, *62-63,* 89, 91, *92-93,* 94, 96, 140, 142
Warmers: bed, *133;* foot, *138-139, 151*
Wartburg castle, Germany, *43;* Luther's stay, 41, 42
Wedding festivities: ball, *85;* beer for, *82;* excesses, 134-135; Luther's, 46-48; Rembrandt's, 113-114; at village church, *26-27*
Weinsberg, Germany: peasant uprising, 66-67
Weisenau monastery, Germany: attack, 67
Werff, Adrian van der, 93-94, 96
West India Company, Dutch, 105, 125; Behaim in, 127-128
Whaling industry: Dutch, *102-103*
William, Prince (Orange), 10, 64, 80, 84-86, 89-94, *91,* 96; and Antwerp unrest, 87, 89-90; departure from Netherlands, 90; Egmont's meeting with, 88-89; and Huguenots, 91; and Leiden siege, 92-94, 96; marriages, 85, 90, 96; murder, 96-97; and Sea Beggars, 90-91, 94, 96
William II, Prince (Orange): death, effect of, 134
William III, Prince (Orange), 11, 140-141, 148, 149
Windmills: Dutch use of, *100-101, 129*
Witches, accused: burning of, *28-29*
Witt, Johan de, 134, 141
Wittenberg, Germany, 25, 27; bonfire, *34-35;* door of church, *16,* 17; marriage of Luthers in, 46-48; order restored to, 44-45; preachers trained in, 45; preaching, Luther's, 31, *40-41,* 44; saints' relics, 27-28; Sastrows in, 73-74; upheavals in, 42, 44
Wolgemut, Michael, 54
Women: breast-feeding, *47,* 150, *151;* burned as witches, *28-29;* businesses, *50-51,* 145; camp followers, 76-77; nuns, *30,* 45, 46. *See also* Dutchwomen; *and individual names*
Worms, Diet of (1521), 36, 39; Edict of Worms, 42, 44, 45
Worms, Germany: Luther in, 36, *39-40*
Wtenbogaert, Joannes, 109, 110

TIME LIFE BOOKS

Time-Life Books is a division of Time Life Inc.

TIME LIFE INC.
PRESIDENT and CEO: George Artandi

TIME-LIFE BOOKS
PUBLISHER/MANAGING EDITOR: Neil Kagan
SENIOR VICE PRESIDENT, MARKETING:
Joseph A. Kuna
VICE PRESIDENT, NEW PRODUCT
DEVELOPMENT: Amy Golden

What Life Was Like ®
IN EUROPE'S GOLDEN AGE

EDITOR: Denise Dersin
DIRECTOR, NEW PRODUCT DEVELOPMENT:
Elizabeth D. Ward
DIRECTOR OF MARKETING: Pamela R. Farrell

Deputy Editor: Marion Ferguson Briggs
Art Director: Alan Pitts
Text Editor: Jarelle S. Stein
Associate Editor/Research and Writing:
Sharon Kurtz Thompson
Senior Copyeditor: Mary Beth Oelkers-Keegan
Technical Art Specialist: John Drummond
Photo Coordinator: David Herod
Editorial Assistant: Christine Higgins

Special Contributors: Ronald H. Bailey, Roberta Conlan, Ellen Galford (chapter text); Gaye Brown, Stacy W. Hoffhaus, Jane Martin, Marilyn Murphy Terrell, Elizabeth Thompson (research-writing); Henk Boute, K. Ginger Crockett, Holly Downen, Sarah L. Evans, Beth Levin (research); Constance Buchanan (editing); Lina Baber Burton (glossary); Barbara L. Klein (index and overread).

Correspondents: Christine Hinze (London), Christina Lieberman (New York), Maria Vincenza Aloisi (Paris). Valuable assistance was also provided by Elizabeth Kramer-Singh, Angelika Lemmer (Bonn).

Director of Finance: Christopher Hearing
Directors of Book Production: Marjann Caldwell, Patricia Pascale
Director of Publishing Technology: Betsi McGrath
Director of Photography and Research: John Conrad Weiser
Director of Editorial Administration: Barbara Levitt
Manager, Technical Services: Anne Topp
Senior Production Manager: Ken Sabol
Production Manager: Virginia Reardon
Quality Assurance Manager: James King
Chief Librarian: Louise D. Forstall

Separations by the Time-Life Imaging Department

Consultant:
Steven Ozment is McLean Professor of Ancient and Modern History at Harvard University and has taught Western civilization at Yale, Harvard, and Stanford. Five of his 10 books have been History Book Club selections, and the *Age of Reform, 1250-1550,* won the Schaff History Prize and was a finalist for the 1981 National Book Award. His most recent books are *The Bürgermeister's Daughter: Scandal in a Sixteenth Century German Town* (1996) and *Flesh and Spirit: A Study of Private Life in Early Modern Germany* (1999).

School and library distribution by Time-Life Education, P.O. Box 85026, Richmond, Virginia 23285-5026.

TIME-LIFE is a trademark of Time Warner Inc. U.S.A.

Library of Congress Cataloging-in-Publication Data
What life was like in Europe's Golden Age: northern Europe, AD 1500-1675 / by the editors of Time-Life Books.
    p. cm. —   (What life was like series; 15)
    Includes bibliographical references (p.) and index.
    ISBN 0-7835-5464-8
    1. Europe, Northern—Civilization. 2. Europe, Northern—Social life and customs. 3. Arts, Modern—17th century—Europe, Northern. 4. Arts, European. 5. Europe, Northern—Intellectual life. 6. Europe—social conditions—16th century. I. Time-Life Books. II. Series.
DL30.W43 1999   99-36176
948'.04—dc21   CIP

This volume is one in a series on world history that uses contemporary art, artifacts, and personal accounts to create an intimate portrait of daily life in the past.

Other volumes included in the *What Life Was Like* series:

On the Banks of the Nile: Egypt, 3050-30 BC
In the Age of Chivalry: Medieval Europe, AD 800-1500
When Rome Ruled the World: The Roman Empire, 100 BC-AD 200
At the Dawn of Democracy: Classical Athens, 525-322 BC
When Longships Sailed: Vikings, AD 800-1100
Among Druids and High Kings: Celtic Ireland, AD 400-1200
In the Realm of Elizabeth: England, AD 1533-1603
Amid Splendor and Intrigue: Byzantine Empire, AD 330-1453
In the Land of the Dragon: Imperial China, AD 960-1368
In the Time of War and Peace: Imperial Russia, AD 1696-1917
In the Jewel in the Crown: British India, AD 1600-1905
At the Rebirth of Genius: Renaissance Italy, AD 1400-1550
Among Samurai and Shoguns: Japan, AD 1000-1700
During the Age of Reason: France, AD 1660-1800

Other Publications:
HISTORY
Our American Century
World War II
The American Story
Voices of the Civil War
The American Indians
Lost Civilizations
Mysteries of the Unknown
Time Frame
The Civil War
Cultural Atlas

COOKING
Weight Watchers® Smart Choice Recipe Collection
Great Taste~Low Fat
Williams-Sonoma Kitchen Library

SCIENCE/NATURE
Voyage Through the Universe

DO IT YOURSELF
Total Golf
How to Fix It
The Time-Life Complete Gardener
Home Repair and Improvement
The Art of Woodworking

TIME-LIFE KIDS
Student Library
Library of First Questions and Answers
A Child's First Library of Learning
I Love Math
Nature Company Discoveries
Understanding Science & Nature

For information on and a full description of any of the Time-Life Books series listed above, please call 1-800-621-7026 or write:

Reader Information
Time-Life Customer Service
P.O. Box C-32068
Richmond, Virginia 23261-2068